The Personal Social Services: An outside view

Alvin L Schorr

July 1992

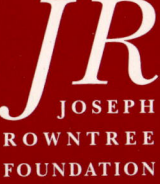

Contents

Introduction 3

1
Background 5

2
Clients and their resources 8

3
The economic environment 12

4
Funding 19

5
'Cognitive dissonance' 22

6
The Children Act and child abuse 32

7
Cost-effectiveness, assessment and care management in community care 35

8
Brinksmanship in administration 41

9
Conclusion: The declining slope 46

10
Recommendations 47

Notes 53

Introduction

In the last years there has been plentiful comment, both cogent and trenchant, on the personal social services (PSS). Some of it has derived from ideological or political views. I do not deny ideological views of my own; the denial would not survive a reading of my published works. However, I have been removed from the development of the British social service departments, and may bring to them some freshness of view and distance from vested interest.

This report does not attempt to comment on every major development, and it is not linear. A number of subjects are selected for comment which, if the reader will suffer them, should come together in the end in a coherent judgement about the current development of the PSS. These subjects are:

1. Background.
2. The PSS clientele and their resources.
3. The economic environment of the PSS.
4. Funding.
5. 'Cognitive dissonance' in the personal social services.
6. The Children Act and child abuse.
7. Cost effectiveness, assessment and care management in community care.
8. Brinksmanship in administration and conclusion.
9. Recommendations.

As they go along readers may notice that, though much has been absorbed, British usages are not scrupulously observed. In tune with the times, the style may be called 'mixed lexicography'. If in the end this is all I have to apologise for, we shall be in good shape. In the preface to a book almost thirty years ago (**1**), Richard Titmuss said of me that I had "written with candour and politeness: sure signs that he came to feel at home in Britain and involved himself in our social discontents. His adversary is not a nation or a class but a human condition." These are the standards to which I aspire.

To keep no secrets, the final view here is that too much has been laid on the personal social services; and they were already overburdened. Inadequate funding is only one aspect of the problem. In some part of their heads, literally all who are involved with these services seem to know this. In some other part of their heads, gallantly and with marked talent, many persevere in thinking through how to do what is asked of them. The overload holds dangers for the PSS that reach beyond the simple possibility that they will not be able to carry out the new responsibilities.

Too much has been laid on an already overburdened service

The personal social services

Acknowledgements

In doing this work, I have visited social service departments and universities, have become familiar with what the Griffiths report called a "formidably voluminous literature" — a phrase for which I developed deep appreciation — and have talked to, certainly, a hundred officials, analysts and experts. The generosity and openness of very busy people much exceeded my expectations.

I have had the advantage of comments on a draft report from Brian Abel Smith, M Ashley Miller, Sir Peter Barclay, Sir Charles Carter, David Donnison, Colin Godber, Sir Roy Griffiths, Rupert Hughes, Robin Huws Jones, Jane Lewis, Janet Lewis, Jan Pahl, J N Morris, Robert Pinker, Hazel Qureshi, Jane Streather, Gwen Swire and Peter Westland.

A small group of experts convened at the invitation of the National Institute for Social Work to discuss a draft of this report. They included Linda Challis, Bob Holman, Michael Oliver, Gillian Parker and Gerald Wistow and Tessa Harding chaired the meeting. All of this was enormously helpful. In the end, of course, I do not necessarily agree with those who have commented or they with me and I alone am responsible for what this report says.

Finally, I must acknowledge assistance and support provided by the National Institute for Social Work, which gave me space, tea, warm interest without interference, and access to what must surely be the most user-friendly library and library staff in the western world. Support of this work by the Joseph Rowntree Foundation is gratefully acknowledged.

Background

The Seebohm Committee undertook its work at a time which lay, as it turned out, between periods of welfare state expansion and contraction. In her little book about 'creation', Joan Cooper wrote "that the process of policymaking is untidy, unpredictable and likely to follow rather than anticipate the realities of social change" (**1**). So it appears to have been with the creation of the personal social services: its successes were a product of the time it was capping, its important failures a product of changes that were not foreseen.

Successes included the creation of a unified department which, for a time at least, attracted increased resources; resolution of the problem of divided responsibility for children at risk; more attention to mentally ill and handicapped people; and greater weight to generic as opposed to specialised service. For the profession of social work, it provided a career structure, improved status and compensation, and the basis for common training for social workers.

There was criticism even at the beginning. Equality, if it was implicit in the Committee report was not explicitly an objective (**2**). Indeed, there was no sense of coherent philosophy; for example, a universal approach was plainly in mind but was not addressed centrally. The thrust was pragmatic, addressing structure and organisation. Then, in his press conference launching the report, Frederic (later Lord) Seebohm, said that the changes are "not going to cost money, or very little". Although Lord Seebohm appears to have held to the view that the departments had to make better use of the resources they had, it was not many years before he was himself pointing to the great pressure on the PSS (**3**).

So failures included an inadequate claim on resources. After a spurt of expenditure on the departments in the early 1970s, real growth in funding slowed (**4**). That this took place in a climate of declining local government spending compounded the problem. With planned, severe fiscal restraint in the 1980s, PSS were poorly situated to cope with what turned out to be swelling needs or demands for service.

The tension between generic and specialist practice is a classical issue in any healing profession and, in social work, reaches back in a straight line to issues confronted in the social administration department of LSE in the 1950s (**5**). Seeing fragmentation of the social services and, indeed, of families receiving service as the greater problem, the Seebohm Committee undertook to press for a more generic approach. Now, the PSS are moving to an emphasis on specialism, at least partly in an effort to cope with child abuse — an issue that assumed prominence after 1971. We shall be discussing this further along.

Community work, which the Seebohm Committee had emphasised, came to seem even more important as time went by. The departments had not moved strongly to community care. This contributed to a twenty year debate, marked by the Barclay and Griffiths reports (**6**), about what community means and what new steps should be taken. It can hardly be doubted that the National Health Service and Community Care Act, *prescribing* implementation of community care, was propelled by rising central government costs for residential care — for elderly people, in particular. As Tessa Jowell writes, "community care is always *subordinate* to other policy agendas" (**7**).

The PSS are moving towards specialism

The personal social services

Demographic changes created undreamt-of demands for services

These are the major social forces that overtook the personal social service departments.

• They were conceived in a period of social optimism, such as may be hard to imagine for those who do not recall it. With national wealth and government revenues growing, there was a widespread view that the state can be and is responsible to solve or at least ameliorate the problems of underprivileged people. The view was "based on a collectivist approach which accepts that the state is responsible" (**8**). As problems seemed to resist solution, optimism faded; as a market ideology superseded the collective spirit, the drive weakened.

• Ideology is not just a climate. For some years during the Thatcher government, the *basic* structure of the welfare state appeared to be unaltered. In 1988, however, education, health and local government finance were changed in ways that led Howard Glennerster to describe them as "the most significant break in the incrementalist tradition of social policy-making that we have seen" since Beveridge (**9**). In particular, the PSS were affected by a struggle for control between central and local government, which local government was bound to lose, of course.

• Social and demographic changes — most prominently the increase in the number of single parent families and in the numbers of elderly and very elderly people — created demands for care and service that had not been dreamt of. A concurrent decline in the birth rate will, in time, compound one problem of care: there will be even fewer adults in their middle years to care for and contribute to the support of the increased number of elderly people.

• Shortly after the social service departments were organised or reorganised in 1971, the Maria Colwell inquiry foreshadowed a steady stream of further inquiries and rising public indignation about child abuse. The public reaction was an exception to deepening social pessimism. There seemed to be a view that more responsible or more skilful social work or reformed laws would halt what was thought of as an alarming, new development.

• Overlying all was an economic downturn, creating new cohorts of poor people — the newly unemployed, for example (**10**) — new priorities about what the government should attend to, and direct pressure to control expenditures of the personal social service departments and for the kind of people who are their clientele. As one effect, means-testing — never dead — gained new charm in comparison with the somewhat abstract benefits of universalism.

I offer this rapid review of organisational and social change to make two introductory points.

First, the policies that were prescribed for the social service departments reflected the climate and the needs of the 1960s and, arguably, the early 1970s. There may have been vision, but it did not encompass a sweeping change in government, social pessimism, economic downturn in the mid-1970s and late 1980s and family change, nor could it reasonably be expected to do so. Only seers would have known about all this in advance; their allegories might have sold but their

Background

policies would not have been adopted.

Second, the personal social service departments are not, more than any branch of government, excused from seeing at least a little way ahead. Still, one has to grasp the scope and variety of the forces with which they dealt and are dealing — largely beyond their remit or capacity to influence in any way. We will have more to say about this matter of capacity.

2 Clients and their resources

Financial resources

The most striking characteristics that clients of the personal social services have in common are poverty and deprivation. Often this is not mentioned, possibly because the social services are said to be based on universalistic principles. Still, everyone in the business knows it. One survey after another shows that clients are unemployed or, to observe a technical distinction, not employed — that is, not working and not seeking work. Perhaps half receive income support; as many as 80 per cent have incomes at or below income support levels (**1**).

Surveys also reveal *why* the PSS are dealing with a predominantly low income population. The elderly seek services; they tend to be poor (**2**). Lone mothers and their children are prominent as clients; commonly, they are poor (**3**). People disabled in one way and another are among clients; they tend to be poor (**4**). Homeless youths and the homeless in general are clients; obviously, most of them are poor. These are classes of people who seek personal social services for the very reasons that make them poor. Elderly people, lone mothers, and the disabled are impoverished by the same characteristic that leads them to seek help — frailty and retirement, only one adult in the family, and so forth.

However, children entering the care of PSS also tend to be poor. For example, of 5 to 9 year olds in families receiving income support, 1 in 10 is admitted to care, but of the same age group *not* on income support, the chances of being admitted to care are 1 in 7,000 (**5**). "Financial poverty is a dominant factor in admitting children to care," one study reports (**6**). One has to grasp that people with decent income manage to avoid having a child enter care. Poorer people try to do the same, but they do not have the financial resources and status to win out. It is true also of elderly people that they are likely not to use public services if they can pay for care (**7**). In short, the PSS are regarded as stigmatising, despite the early aim for a universal approach; and social class carries weight (**8**). What else is new!

I take pains to report what everybody knows about the departments' clients in order to point to several implications.

First, the guidance surrounding recent legislation has been about partnership and participation. As PSS clients are poor, however, they are not equal partners in a care management or child care case conference. They find themselves in an alien environment; habits of politeness and deference subvert them (see Section 5).

A second implication is about financing. Both budgetary stringency and changes in arrangements for government financing have created heated competition for funds among education, housing and social service departments, not to mention other public services. In this struggle against constituencies that are largely middle class, the constituency of the social service departments is very weak. Not only are poor people politically weak, sociologically, it is well understood that the professionals who deal with poor people tend to be politically weak. The PSS maintained their position against middle class competition for some years (**9**), but with current constraints unequal political power is likely to translate into under-financing.

A third implication has to do with other-than financial resources of poor people, and this requires some paragraphs of its own.

The most striking characteristics clients share are poverty and deprivation

Clients and their resources

Family and social resources

The main thrust of the NHS and Community Care Act lies in diverting the elderly and other adults from residential care to care that can be provided by families and other informal carers — assisted, when desirable and feasible, by local authority services. To some extent, it appears that administration of the Children Act may be influenced by this philosophical bent, an inclination that can be supported — if one wants to read it this way — by the Act's emphasis on parental responsibility and minimum intervention.

These Acts represent the explicit objectives of the government during the past decade, and their administration will certainly be influenced by these objectives. Janet Finch has observed that the objective is "... to encourage us all to return to ... acknowledging the duty to support our relatives and act accordingly" (**10**). If the PSS are more exactly dealing with poor people than with the general population, it is important to ask the extent to which poor people have the kind of resources that are to be relied upon.

At least partly in response to steadily rising interest in community care over the past twenty years, research is now available that makes it possible to unravel some of the complex strands of informal care. By and large, serious care is provided by family members — women more often than men, though men are not out of the picture. There has been some dispute about the role of men. It appears that men provide supportive help — moral support, as one report says (**11**) — to women, who take the main responsibility. Men become so-called 'sole carers' when it is their wife who needs care.

There is a good deal of caring in Britain (depending on what one expects, of course) — six million adults who were taking substantial responsibility in 1985. Neighbours and friends are not nearly so involved as family, as Philip Abrams and others have emphasised (**12**). Abrams pointed to "an antithesis ... between neighbourhood care as sociability and neighbourhood care as service delivery" (**13**). Neighbourhood networks, he observed, were most available when directed to political ends (**14**).

In short, neighbourhood and friends may be counted on in emergencies, for conversation (not an inconsiderable contribution), or for small offices of tenderness, but the substantial burden is assumed by one person; generally this is a close family member, generally a woman. Almost two-thirds of carers spend twenty hours a week or more at caring; two-thirds of *them* would find it difficult if not impossible to arrange for a substitute if they needed time off (**15**).

Informal care within the family is not a simple matter of altruism, proffered or not proffered. In some fashion the role of carer is settled within a family over what may be a long period of time (because, for example, the person selected is unmarried or not employed) and the role is accepted by the carer for reasons that quite often include implicit or explicit expectation of gain (**16**).

The sense of love or responsibility that may be involved in giving care is mixed with a feeling that past favours are being returned, or current or future favours will be rendered. It is mixed also with the expectation that, in a market economy, payment is due for some kinds of services (**17**) and a conviction that the roles of state and family are distinguishable. While some things are expected from family,

Serious care is provided by family members

The personal social services

others are expected from the state (**18**). In the end, "sentiment mixes with practical advantage and a complex understanding is arrived at in which expectation of inheritance, practical services, concern, and love are balanced and harmonized" (**19**).

Now, it must be clear on the face of it that the evolution and negotiation that go on in a poor family is different from that in a middle class family. There is no inheritance to speak of; there are no real resources to offer in reciprocation. In addition, the potential carer is beset and besieged by her own problems. An example is the unemployed man who couldn't go shopping for his mother because he didn't have petrol for his car or the money to buy it (**20**).

Thus, for poor families there may be love and concern; there is frequently a sense of responsibility; but these solidify into caring — when they do — at the edge of the family's capacities.

Moreover, it is in the nature of the dynamics of poverty that poor families do not have as extensive social networks as families that are better off. The problems that lead to poverty turn them inward and clip the social networks that they may have had. In some measure this must be obvious, but the mechanisms which do this to the unemployed, for example, have been carefully elaborated. Marie Jahoda identifies five elements of rootedness that are disturbed or destroyed by unemployment. These are "the experience [or structuring] of time, the reduction of social contacts, the lack of participation in collective purposes, the absence of an acceptable status and its consequences for personal identity, and the absence of regular activity" (**21**).

The potential carer is beset by her own problems

In fact, one study after another names aspects of constricted networks from which the poor suffer. They complain of isolation and absence of social contact and anyone to talk to (**22**). Their carers are ill; they "cry for respite" (**23**). Although overall population figures are much more modest, indications are that among families connected with PSS, as many as half the carers are themselves older than 65 and not a few with primary responsibility for caring are children less than 14 years old (**24**).

Here and there, a study notes that poor families *could* name social contacts, but they had already been refused help or expected to be refused (**25**). Elderly people, in particular, are sometimes *not willing* to ask for help. They are well aware of problems that their children are having, and they are afraid that asking for help will lead to estrangement. They would rather suffer discomfort or deprivation than risk disturbing these relationships (**26**).

Having catalogued all this, one must say that, nevertheless, often the poor do help one another; it is impressive that they do. They do not have money to give nor much in the way of energy; they give what they can. In extremity, for usually it is not what the carer or cared-for wants to do, they share living quarters (**27**). To review in two sentences: the clients of the personal social services are mainly poor people, and the poor do not have social or family resources to spare. On the contrary, what they are giving now is given with great difficulty.

Will community care policies, stringently applied, as they may be, bring forth resources that have not so far been evident? Janet Finch comments:

Clients and their resources

There have been several times during the last two centuries when governments have tightened the screws, to try to ensure that people relied on their families rather than on the state for financial assistance: the creation of the New Poor Law in 1834; the tightening of Poor Law regulations in the late nineteenth century; the creation of the household means test for unemployed people in the 1930s. The historical evidence suggests that...the measures were less successful than their hard-line advocates would have wished... When government was attempting to impose a version of family responsibilities which people regarded as unreasonable, many responded by developing avoidance strategies: moving to another household, losing touch with their relatives, cheating the system ... It seems that it is not in the power of governments straight-forwardly to manipulate what we do for our relatives, let alone what we believe to be proper. (28)

A reading of the experience with American policy with respect to the responsibility of relatives, which was very tough indeed for many years, would come to a similar conclusion.

Little was produced for the state in the way of increased contributions, though much pain and travail resulted for poor people. The government's gain, such as it was, lay in deterring people from applying for benefits to which they were legally entitled (**29**).

One must conclude that, whether deliberately or inadvertently, with its policies for community care the government is turning from cutting back on social security for poor people to squeezing their relationships and living arrangements. If it were to work as intended, this policy too might save government money. In all likelihood, it will not work and will not save money, but poor people will feel it, of course. This is not to say that a government policy of capping expenditures will not save money, but that is a different matter.

Part of the rationale for cutting back on social security rests in arguments that payment of benefits interferes with incentive to work. But what is the rationale for pulling and hauling at the way poor people live?

It should, perhaps, be made explicit that there is a profound gender issue here. In general, observations about poor people have clear implications for women and minorities of various sorts, who are over-represented among the poor. In addition to this, however, the evidence is and the chances are that women will *continue* to do the caring — the sole caring, the large part of the caring, other trends towards equality between the sexes notwithstanding (**30**). Among the poor, poor women in particular will feel the consequences of the community care policy.

All of this could, of course, be transformed by the commitment of substantial new government financing *to create* community care services, as *Caring for People* more or less promises. There appears to be a view that such financing can be provided by concomitant savings in the cost of residential care. This is likely to happen when, in the Arab phrase, apricots bloom in the desert. (See Sections 4 and 7.)

Poor women in particular will feel the consequences of community care

3

The economic environment

The PSS are powerfully influenced by over-arching economic policy

The economic environment

It is for PSS as it would be if Noah thought he could correct the flood by riding it out. The problem was created higher up, and he could only struggle to survive and pray for reprieve. Similarly, PSS are being rained on by the economy and its problems and institutions. I offer an example.

Conventional wisdom has it that residential care of elderly people expands because of a longer life span, a variety of changes in family relationships, and the so-called 'perverse incentive' in social security (that is, social security payment for residential care). Yet, these are not all.

A powerful force with respect to residential care is the relationship of the income of elderly people to average income; looming large among its determinants is the level of retirement pensions. The connection is evident over the last hundred years or more. For example, between 1870 and 1890 Poor Law Pensions were cut back radically by reformers seeking to replace the pensions with family maintenance and workhouse care. The proportion of elderly people in institutions promptly rose (**1**).

Again, the introduction of the Old Age Pension of 1908 led directly to a decline in age-specific rates of residential care (**2**). "The lesson ... from history," writes David Thomson, "is that the declining true value of pensions in the 1950s, 1960s and 1970s is the cause of the rising number of elderly in institutions" (**3**).

It is not simply the proportion of elderly people in residential care that is convincing. The relative fates of men and women (that is, whether women are more or less likely than men to be in residential care) have been tied directly to which sex was receiving more favourable treatment under pension laws (**4**). For fifty years, the age-specific proportion in residential care has been rising faster for women than for men, speculatively at least because men were getting occupational pensions and women were not (**5**).

The recent rapid growth in residential care — now equivalent to 50 per cent of local authority spending on social services — is itself an indicator of financial need. Similarly, a British Medical Association report observes that it is "a lack of alternatives that [has led] many of the voluntary patients to seek hospital care" (**6**).

For what it is worth, American experience accords with these observations. Despite relevant developments since the 1960s that were similar to Britain's, including extensive government payment for residential care, the proportion of elderly Americans in such care has barely increased (**7**). In this period, however, the income of elderly people relative to younger people in the United States improved dramatically, in large measure because of improvements in social security.

It is well understood that elderly people do not like to enter residential care and will not do so if they are afforded a reasonable alternative. But they have to have enough to live on.

The experience of elderly people over the years is offered to illustrate the point that recourse by the poor to personal social services is not simply determined by the legislation or policies that are laid on the PSS. The work and clientele of the personal social services are powerfully influenced by over-arching economic policy. It may, therefore, be useful to review what has been happening in these institutions — in particular, in social security, housing, and employment.

The economic environment

Social security

Among various ways of defining poverty are the number of people who receive income-related social security benefits, the number below 50 per cent of average income, the number who lack what the general public regards as necessities and the gap between those with the least and those with the most income (**8**). It is possible to argue which, if any of these, most accurately counts 'poverty'. By any definition, however, the number who are poor has *more than doubled* in the last ten or twelve years and they are now *more severely poor.*

That this was happening even as real income was rising for the general population is not entirely so puzzling. Real disposable income grew by more than 30 per cent between 1979 and 1988 for the average family but real income (after housing costs) for the poorest tenth of the population rose by only 2 per cent (**9**). Thus — a widely remarked phenomenon — the living standard of the average family improves but the standard of the average poor family remains the same or, for selected groups, even declines.

Does increasing inequality matter if the poorest retain approximately the same real income? Apparently it does. Inequality in itself makes it difficult to compete in buying power (**10**) — a plausible finding, if one thinks about it; indeed, inequality affects life expectancy *for everyone* (**11**) and it affects the public perception of what poverty is. In 1983, for example, 7.5 million people had lacked three publicly defined necessities; by 1990, the figure was 11 million (**12**). One of the necessities that poor children and their parents lacked was enough to eat every day of the month (**13**).

Social security provides more than two-thirds of the income of the poorest fifth of the population (**14**). Once people have suffered a problem that interferes with income (for example, unemployment, retirement, or disability), social security becomes *the major determinant* of their level of living.

A number of changes in social security have come to public attention, but many changes appear to affect small groups of people and go unnoticed. The *central* observation to make about such changes is that there have been many more than have come to public attention; their compound effect is a grave deterioration in the level of living of the poorest 20 per cent of the population.

By 1989, limiting himself to the social security changes that affected the unemployed, A B Atkinson catalogued 36 changes to national insurance, supplementary benefit/income support, and housing benefit — for example, abolition of the earnings-related supplement, effective in 1982; abolition of child additions by 1984; and narrowing the definition of voluntary redundancy from 1985 (**15**). Casting a somewhat wider net but still limited to the unemployed, a group at the University of Edinburgh counted fifty such changes (**16**).

Estimating the cost to the unemployed of just 13 of the changes, Atkinson reports that they would otherwise "have received £510 million more than under the present policy …" (**17**). Dealing with social security in general, Peter Townsend estimates that as much as £7 to £8 billion more would have been spent on benefits in 1989 if rules had remained unchanged since 1979 (**18**). Approaching the issue even more broadly, John Hills observes that, between 1978-79 and 1988-89, "cuts in direct taxes have entirely been paid for by cuts in the generosity of benefits. There has been a

The number of poor has more than doubled in the last twelve years

The personal social services

major redistribution from those on low incomes to the better off." If taxes and benefits had remained unchanged and benefit levels had improved in line with national growth, benefit levels in 1988 would have been 164 per cent higher! (**19**).

The elderly

Along with the losers, a minority among social security beneficiaries have gained from the changes, and there is a general impression that elderly people have done well. The basic pension for the retired went up about 10 per cent in real money between 1974 and 1988; with payment of SERPS included, in about the same period the average pension went from £32 to £45 per week (**20**). *On average,* the ratio in disposable income between retired and working households improved substantially (**21**).

The difficulty, once again, is that there is a very considerable degree of inequality *among* elderly people; the poorest 20 per cent had virtually no non-benefit income in 1986; the most prosperous 20 per cent had £11,704 per year (**22**). Further, the poorest were benefiting very little from SERPS; and the basic pension, though it has improved in real money, has declined by 20 per cent in relation to average earnings (1978 to 1991) (**23**). As a result, 1.8 million single pensioners, almost half of all single pensioners and the most likely candidates for residential or community care, were poor in 1988 (**24**). For them, at any rate, the substantial boost for which Thomson asked has not been forthcoming.

Conspicuous among government measures which undermine the income of elderly people was the decision in 1980 to uprate the retirement pension in response to cost of living alone, cutting it loose from changes in earnings level. Also a serious factor is the rise in unemployment level, which is presumably responsible for the considerable decline over the last two decades in the proportion of elderly at paid work. Third, cuts in housing benefit appear to have played a role in increasing the number of poor pensioners (**25**). Finally, a variety of changes in administrative practice, especially with regard to hospital care and discharge and payment for residential care, deprive elderly people of benefits or reduce their levels (**26**).

The losers

Prominent losers in the economic and social security changes of the 1980s were the unemployed — over the decade, almost doubling as a proportion of the low-income population — and lone parents with children (**27**).

A little has already been said about the benefits of the unemployed and, though it will hold no surprises, something should be said about children. Three million children, 25 per cent of all children, were poor in 1988. Why so many?

Child benefit was frozen for three years and, despite a recent rise, in real terms is still £2 a week less than its 1977 level (**28**). As for its relation to the average wage, the benefit for a second child, for example, has declined by 30 per cent since 1979 (**29**). This is a product of the 1980 government decision about benefit uprating noted just above.

In the changeover from supplementary benefit to income support in 1988, to take Hammersmith and Fulham as a local example, 3,400 claimants gained benefit and 9,000 lost it (**30**). In real terms, income support for a lone

There is considerable inequality among elderly people

The economic environment

parent with one young child has declined by about £1 a week (**31**). The introduction of the Social Fund meant the withdrawal of £300 million a year from the poor, and "there is a clear possibility that loans might increase hardship among claimants ..." (**32**). And so on, at whatever length one can bear.

Housing

Homelessness in Britain is most visible on the ground, as one may say. Homelessness for families doubled between 1980 and 1990. During the 1980s, an average of 300,000 people a year — half of them children — were registered as homeless by local authorities (**33**). Young people under 25 years of age are conspicuous among the homeless. As many as one-third of them had been in the care of local authorities (**34**).

Homelessness is only the readily visible evidence of housing shortage; there are other effects as well. Average housing quality had been improving for years but, in the 1980s, the numbers "that were unfit or in 'serious' disrepair remained stubbornly high, standing at" about 1 million each (**35**). Crowding is certainly increasing as renters cannot pay, new families cannot find housing, and the numbers of owners whose homes are repossessed rises towards 80,000 to 100,000 a year (**36**).

Moreover, maintaining housing places a severe strain on the budgets of homeowners, even if they are employed. Simply paying the mortgage takes one-third or more of their net income, on the average (**37**), and an owned home imposes other expenses as well.

Finally, an effect of lack of housing is to keep people in unsuitable arrangements; patients who should go home are in mental hospitals, for example (**38**).

Causes of the housing problem were summed up as follows by John Greve:

The overriding cause of homelessness is the critical and growing shortage of affordable rental housing. Three key and mutually reinforcing factors, which have developed strongly since 1979, have contributed to the shortage. They are: the sharp reduction in council building; a massive switch in funding away from new building; the vigorously promoted 'Right to Buy' policy. (**39**)

Greve's first and third factors are very important, but the massive switch in funding away from new building is fundamental to the problem that is now presented. Operating on a "simple textbook [economic] model" (**40**) the government freed housing finance of restraint, triggering a sharp inflation, so that home prices rose much more rapidly than general prices. Classical theory was, or was thought to be, that builders and investors would see an opportunity and enter this market. Unfortunately, as Maclennan writes: "All the estimates confirm the unresponsiveness of housing supply to changing prices." Prices went up, but supply did not respond.

House price inflation was compounded by the appearance on the housing market of the baby-boom generation. At the same time, the number of poor people was increasing and income inequality was growing — a phenomenon that causes homelessness *even in the absence of poverty* (**41**). The cost of housing much exceeded the capacity of most of the population to pay for it. Building and financial

Homelessness for families doubled between 1980 and 1990

The personal social services

institutions withdrew. Housing starts, an inadequate 235,000 in 1980, fell to 175,000 in 1991 (**42**).

It was to this unfortunate cycle that the 'Right to Buy' policy added impetus. As local authorities sold housing, they were inclined to turn over proceeds into new council housing. For reasons other than housing production, the government restrained them and new starts for council housing, 86,000 in 1980, fell to 13,000 in 1991 (**43**). Council housing and housing associations had provided virtually the only new rental housing since the Second World War. In the circumstances, private builders were in no way tempted to enter the market, and investment by housing associations in building and rehabilitation also declined markedly (**44**).

Thus, the housing resources available to local authorities decline even as the crisis in housing faces social service departments with mounting requests for accommodation. For some, like people defined as vulnerable and children who have been in care, local authorities are required by law to make provision. In 1989 and 1990, about 200,000 families in England and Wales used temporary accommodation. It is estimated that half a million more homeless families are likely to use temporary accommodation by 1995 (**45**).

Lack of housing only begins a problem that will take its course over years. Crowding combined with withdrawal of housing benefit leads young people to leave home prematurely (**46**). Homeless families and families in temporary accommodation "cannot put down lasting roots" (**47**). People without an address have difficulty finding employment; and extended unemployment is likely to make people unfit for work — particularly young people just starting out. Crowded and homeless families produce more than a 'normal' quota of neglected and abused children.

Re-establishing a home that has been lost, particularly for people who are poor or disabled or elderly, is not so simple as turning the clock back. Furnishings have to be assembled; care has to be assembled; the very family may need to be assembled. For many, once the home is lost they will remain in the residence or foster home until, one way or another, they graduate.

In short, the housing shortage is building a reservoir of demand for PSS that will long outlive the current recession and housing crisis, when and if it is taken in hand.

Employment and unemployment

Unemployment in the UK has fluctuated sharply in the past few years, rising from 5.5 per cent in 1980 to over 13 per cent in 1984 (**48**). Then, for several years unemployment declined — only to climb again in 1990 and 1991. The official unemployment rate is now (March 1992) 9.4 per cent; by the OECD definition, the rate must now exceed that of 1984.

Other aspects of employment and unemployment are especially troubling for the long term. First, even in the period when overall unemployment was declining, the proportion out of work for a year or more 'soared'. The long-term unemployed accounted for one-quarter of all the unemployed in 1979, and one-third in 1990 (**49**). The number of people involved appears to be heading for 1 million.

The government's view is that many of these people are work-shy. An alternative view is that labour market changes leave increasing numbers unqualified for job vacancies or unwilling to work at the poor wages or in the

The number of long-term unemployed appears to be heading for 1 million

The economic environment

poor conditions that are offered (50). Moreover, employers tend not to hire those who have been unemployed for many months if recently unemployed people are available.

It seems clear that wages at the low end of the scale have been declining steadily. Comparing the lowest wage rates for eight European countries (adjusted to compare purchasing power), the UK ranks sixth — ahead only of Spain and Portugal (51). More than 10 million adult workers earn less than the Council of Europe's 'decency threshold' — £5.15 an hour (52). This represents a considerable proportionate increase in numbers since 1979. Earnings of the lowest paid manual worker relative to average earnings are now lower than at any time since such records were first kept in 1886 (53).

Third, there has been a considerable shift from full- to part-time work. More than two-thirds of the increase in the number of jobs between 1983 and 1990 was expansion of part-time work. These changes have been under way for several decades and, by 1990, part-time and other so-called peripheral work (temporary work, self employment) accounted for well over a third of the labour force (54).

One can regard these developments with cheer or with gloom. On the one hand, they provide flexibility for women, who are the very large majority of part-time workers, and for others whom flexibility suits; and employers have a cheaper work force that can more readily be expanded and contracted. On the other hand, pay is lower by the hour in part-time than in full-time work, fringe benefits poor or non-existent and tenure insecure.

There is an obvious overlap between the spread of peripheral work and the steady deterioration of low-pay wage scales. There is an overlap too with the groups of people who tend to make out badly in the labour market — women, youths, and minorities (55). That is, they are pre-eminently the ones who — when they can get work — work part-time, for lower pay, and with poorer work conditions. It has been argued that the long-term unemployed are not wanted by employers and so are not a factor in depressing wages, but the large pool of short-term unemployed, part-time, and temporary workers is another matter.

The important point here is that this parlous situation reflects long-term trends with respect to which the government is only one player, although a critical one. The government has made it clear that it seeks to depress wages or keep them down in order to be able to compete on the world market and avoid job losses. Therefore, over the years, it has removed pay protection for the young and unskilled, has limited the purview of wage councils and has opposed a minimum wage. Probably more consequential, however, has been the decline of manufacturing in Britain and the continuous expansion of the service industries — which lend themselves so much more readily to peripheral workers and low pay.

One could enter into a considerable argument — and I do not propose to do that — about the strategies of British business and government with respect to the economy and employment. The point here is narrower: long-term trends in industry and employment and government policy with respect to them, accentuated by the recession, to be sure, place terrific strain on large numbers of people,

Wages at the low end of the scale have declined steadily

The personal social services

producing increases in poverty that have been noted, contributing to problems about securing housing, and making more and more people dependent on social security — particularly on means-tested social security. This means more work for PSS, unless they find evasive strategies, as they may well do.

Coming out of the recession, when that happens, will moderate but not end these pressures. Low pay, a third of the work force engaged in peripheral work, 1 million workers unemployed for a year or more: these are deep-seated economic, not to say social problems and they will create people-problems with which the social service departments will be expected to deal.

Concluding comments

In short, social security cutbacks, a housing shortage not readily corrected in the near future, and a transformed employment market of which the same must be said, come together to present millions of families with desperate difficulties.

The material in this section has been presented broadly and statistically, but it is not possible to think about it very long without realising how severe the pressures are, family by family. It is the very same family that contends with an unemployed wage earner, a 17 year old who costs money but does not contribute any, rent rises that housing benefit will not cover, and an elderly parent who needs more and more care.

Social security is arranged in such a fashion that the wife's work will bring no increase in income. If they apply to the Social Fund, they may wind up with a debt that will compound their problems. When the family seeks help for the elderly parent, the social service department may seem to wonder why they do not provide more care themselves. It would be a heroic family that did not quarrel, where the youth might not wonder whether he would do himself and everyone a favour to take himself off and where the father did not feel himself a failure and blamed for it. If there are young children, there would be other problems.

Speaking of the views that had guided his work, Albert Einstein once said that God is subtle but not vicious. The system that the economic environment creates for low income people is vicious and not subtle. It not only creates poor people; it pauperises them, seeking out and stripping them of their last resources, forcing youths out of the home who might otherwise have helped, bringing together reluctant family members into one crowded dwelling. Whatever other problems this may create for society, it will create clients and claimants in large numbers for the social services. These departments will be rained upon.

Recovery from recession will moderate not end these pressures

4 Funding

We have referred in passing to anticipated levels of funding for the PSS; it is important to address the issue directly. Disclaiming any intention to comment on resources, the Griffiths Report nevertheless observes that:

> *To talk of policy in matters of care except in the context of available resources and timescales for action owes more to theology than to the purposeful delivery of a caring service. (para. 9)*
>
> *[And] What cannot be acceptable is to allow ambitious policies to be embarked on without the appropriate funds. (para. 38)*

Just so!

Trends in support of the social services have been appraised with great care in *The State of Welfare* and *Great Expectations*, among others (1). Expenditure trends can shift about and seem very abstruse — partly because of the way data are collected and partly depending on where one wants to come out — and it would not be useful to try to work through this here. Based on such analyses, however, it can fairly be said that expenditure on the PSS moved sharply upward for four years after 1971, in constant prices and relative to other social welfare expenditure, and was thereafter more and then much more tightly constrained.

In 1976, the government suggested that a real increase of 2 per cent each year would maintain stability in relation to demographic change and other unspecified pressures. Admittedly a 'very crude estimate', 2 per cent remained the government's yardstick for many years (2) and perhaps it still is. It does seem to have failed to take into account increases in poverty, the cumulative impact of cuts in social security, the increase in single parenthood and in homelessness, the coming out of the closet of child abuse and deeper sensitivity to the relative lack of access by minorities.

These are much to have failed to take into account; nevertheless, until recently, growth in real expenditure approximated the 2 per cent yardstick. It is not surprising then that, in the net, *per capita* provision of social service started to fall in 1976-7, and declined more sharply after 1978-9 (3). In short, the PSS were already seriously underfunded well before the start-up dates of community care and the Children Act.

It cannot be overlooked, and it has consequences that reach beyond financing, that an important element in the issue of expenditure is the government's struggle to bring all local authorities into line with central government policy. This is painfully evident in a new policy that reaches beyond constraining government contributions to placing explicit limits on what local authorities may spend — charge-capping. It took a while for charge-capping really to be felt but for 1991-2, a year in which the Children Act is in effect and community care in a transitional phase, a quarter of all local authorities were budgeted at no more than or less (in real money) than they had spent in the prior year (4).

What is spent or what is delivered does not necessarily reflect what is needed, one way or the other. This question may be approached in a variety of ways — for example, by cataloguing indicators of unmet need among mentally ill, elderly, disabled and other user groups (5). One can call attention to the wide disparity in provision between one locality and another — for example, 273 home helps per 1,000 over 75 years of age in Buckinghamshire compared with

The PSS were underfunded before the start of community care

The personal social services

Authorities lack staff for genuine planning

90 per thousand in Surrey, suggesting that available provision is too low in many places (**6**). Together with the fact that per capita provision has been declining, such indicators reinforce the view that need has not been met, that is, that for fifteen years the PSS have been underfunded.

With a 2 per cent increase or no increase or, indeed, a cutback, how then are PSS to deal with new and additional requirements? In many places, they will find themselves unable to meet statutory requirements — for example, to survey children in need. Common sense sometimes overrides statutes, and very few hard-pressed departments will see much point in discovering children in need for whom they will not have the resources to do anything (**7**). How are the departments to do genuine planning? Genuine planning costs genuine money but, having studied the matter, Howard Glennerster concludes that local authorities do not have nearly enough staff to do the planning job (**8**).

How are PSS to do training, bearing in mind that homehelps are to move into personal care and that social workers and others who are to do care management will need wholly new skills? (**9**) How are PSS to improve the salaries and professionalism of residential child care workers, whose suitability and expertise are at the heart of questions about mistreatment of children in care? (**10**) How will they deal with the "increasingly heavy burden" that HIV and AIDS are bringing to them? (**11**)

How will they consult with users as required? (**12**) Formally, presumably, in a perfunctory and ultimately meaningless manner. Complaint procedures will very likely be established, as the requirement to do so is clear and the methodology bureaucratic. But will formal consultation take place after it becomes evident that complaint procedures proceed more crisply, in a more orderly fashion than any correctives that may be indicated?

Local authorities are required to make available the following personal support services:

Advice, guidance, and counselling
Occupational, social, cultural, recreational facilities
Home help, including laundry facilities
Assistance with travel to use a service
Assistance with holidays
Family centres
Day care for children under five and in need
Appropriate care and supervised activities outside school hours and in school holidays for those in need of any age, who attend school
Accommodation instead of the traditional voluntary reception into care. (**13**)

Much of this will be new to PSS, and the rest represents expansion beyond what they now do. But how? With what?

One who puts these questions is likely quickly to be drawn into discussing the expectation that well over £1,000 million that would otherwise be used to pay for residential care is to be transferred from social security to local authorities. It is a large sum of money, in itself and compared with the £4,000 million-plus total expenditure on PSS. The size of the transfer has seized the imagination of many people, and seems to carry mythic possibilities.

Yet, very little if any of this money will be available to do other than it is now doing. The

Funding

sum to be transferred is to be based on the government's estimate of what would be newly required for residential care in the absence of the new emphasis on community care. Presumably the large majority of these people will enter residential care just as the government estimates. For example, studies indicate that currently only a small minority of elderly people are inappropriately in residential care — 17 per cent *at most* (**14**). The cost for those newly entering residential care will be borne out of the funds transferred to PSS.

Moreover, many now in residential care are topping up their benefit (**15**). Presumably charges will rise even further and local authorities are now to be required to fill the gap, at a cost they estimate at £130 million (**16**). This will mop up any excess that may conceivably develop. As if all this were not enough, social security payments have been available for elderly but not for learning disabled or physically disabled people. Such money is locked up in Health Authorities and it is so far unclear that any or much of it will be transferred to local authorities.

Meanwhile, Health Authorities are discharging patients "quicker and sicker" (**17**). "Today," writes Malcolm Dean, "we have ... still not nearly enough provision to cover the 35,000 lost hospital beds" (**18**). It is clear that there will be candidates for any residential and nursing home beds that are vacated by people now in them.

There is some anxiety that local authorities will spend the social security money on "roads, or schools, or whatever takes their fancy" (**19**). On the whole, that seems to me to be unlikely. The point here is that this money is, for some little time, largely committed to the people now using it and to the most desperate new situations that will arise.

The Griffiths report recommended earmarking ('ringfencing') the funds that would be turned over to local authorities, precisely to conserve these funds for community care. The government rejected this recommendation, observing that it did not wish to erode local authority discretion (**20**). It is an odd argument to come from a government that has been pouring forth guidance which local authorities, at any rate, take to be prescriptive. Sir Roy Griffiths observed that "whereas he designed a four-wheeled vehicle for community care the Government has opted in its wisdom for a three-wheeled vehicle" (**21**).

Whether community care will save money in the longer run is a separable question, and we will deal with it separately. For the purpose here, the answer is not much. In any event, it is in the near term that the PSS must manage the transition to new programming.

In sum, there was not enough money to begin with; "resources are grossly inadequate at a time when local authorities face new responsibilities ..."(**22**); and little that is not pre-committed is being added. In Sir Roy Griffiths' words, adapted, to be sure, ambitious policies have been embarked on without the appropriate funds.

Little funding that is not pre-committed is being added

5 'Cognitive dissonance'

The manager's overriding concern will be budget limitations

"Human beings show a strain towards consistency," Leon Festinger wrote (**1**). When they feel an inconsistency between their behaviour and their views about how they should behave, they exhibit eccentric or pathological behaviour intended to reduce discomfort. He called the phenomenon 'cognitive dissonance'. The PSS are facing cognitive dissonance at an uncomfortably high decibel level. We begin with the question of user choice in community care and children's services.

User choice in community care

The government White Paper, *Caring for People*, speaks of user choice, saying, for example, that the government's approach should:

> *give people a greater individual say in how they live their lives and the services they need to help them to do so.*

> *Promoting choice and independence underlies all the government's proposals. (1.8)*

After this, choice is mentioned only in subordinate clauses or carefully qualified context. For example:

> *It will be [the responsibility of social service authorities] to make maximum possible use of private and voluntary providers, and so increase the available options and widen consumer choice. (1.11)*

In a section captioned 'consumer choice', the White Paper makes it clear that users may choose if their choice is no more expensive or if they are prepared to top up the costs that are allowable (3.7.8, 3.7.9).

There are at least two rather different ways of thinking about choice in community care. One is a market definition: if a broad menu is available of residential care, family and informal helps, home helps, and so forth — some of these provided by local authorities and some not — and the consumer may select, then he or she has a choice. The point here is the menu. A close reading of the White Paper and subsequent guidance suggests that this is the meaning that the government intends.

Yet, true choice depends in turn on whether the care that is preferred will be paid for. For consumers with money to spend, if only to top up government payments, nothing is added by the programme changes. However, low income people who apply to social service departments, must depend on whether the *department* will pay for their choice. This gets to a second definition of choice: the consumer may choose and, to some substantial degree and within reason, the government will pay if the consumer cannot. But this is *not* what the government intends.

One sees this, above all, in White Paper and training material emphasis on the role of the care (or case) manager. The government's support for care managers arises largely, if not solely, from the conviction that they will see that "resources are managed effectively" (**2**). The care manager's overriding concern will be to observe budget limitations, which will translate into selection of the least expensive care options. This may coincide with the user's choice; it may not. Linda Challis explains that the government has not designed a love seat:

'Cognitive dissonance'

> *An increased emphasis on assessment does not bode well for 'choice.' The White Paper seems not to appreciate that choice and assessment do not sit very comfortably together.* (**3**)

For example, the Disability Income Group has expressed itself bluntly about the relation of choice to care managers.

> *The concept of 'care managers' 'to oversee the assessment and re-assessment function and manage the resulting action' is ... highly suspect [they wrote to the Social Services Committee of the House of Commons.] It threatens to add another tier of authority over the individual disabled person, creating an expensive, unnecessary, authoritarian director of community resources. Having little contact with the subjects of his/her overseeing and managing, and no doubt highly trained and qualified, the 'care manager' could dictate the outcome of assessments. Rather than a 'manager', social services authorities should merely supply to the disabled person a 'named person' to ensure that someone is responsible for helping specified disabled people.* (**4**)

Instead, the Disability Income Group supported providing a sum of money to disabled people, permitting the choice customarily provided by being able to pay.

Perhaps it is important to emphasise that the expression of this point of view is not an *ad hoc* reaction to a particular proposal. Rooted in an analysis of social service over the years, it represents a carefully considered view that traditional social services and well-intended overseeing of disabled people foster dependency, whereas disabled people wish to be independent (**5**). In principle, statements of social service and government policy also support the objective of independence.

What transpires about choice is likely to be obscured anyway. Guidance papers suggest a measure of confusion in specifying that the views of the user and carer may be heard separately, as they may differ (**6**). They may, indeed. Is the implication, then, that the care manager is deciding between them? Judgements will be made about the capacities and wishes of the carer as well as the person cared for. Professionals who are involved in assessment will also offer judgements. Some community resources and beds in residences will be readily available; others will not. All this has to come together in the care manager's head, and it will come together under the constraints of money and administrative pressure to avoid expensive care. It may in the end be entirely unclear whether user choices that were reasonably possible have been honoured.

Apart from that, it is so far only a theory that a mixed economy of welfare will provide a broad spectrum of choices. At the very least, success depends upon funding. This is especially so as family carers are under great strain and may be thinking that there will now be *more* provision, and they may be able to choose to use some of it. The government has been vigorous in asserting that it will provide adequate resources (**7**), but it has been indicated above that these assurance appear to bear no relation to reality.

These observations are not intended to question the need to control government

Issues about choice remain obscure

The personal social services

expenditures. The difficulty is rather that it is widely thought, in the PSS and out, that PSS clients are going to be able to choose what they want — within limits, to be sure. For example, Stephen Campbell writes very warmly about community care: "Throughout the land there is agreement about the basic principles. These involve choice..." (8). "The community care changes," says an Association of County Councils briefing paper "give people a greater chance to influence the shape of care available to them" (9). Even critics address community care as if it were meant to let clients choose. Simon Biggs points out, for example, that the care manager and client do not meet as equals, in a position to strike a marketplace bargain (10). Even as he criticises, he assumes that the government is saying that it is going to let people choose, or bargain.

One reason for confusion about choice lies in focusing, as government statements have consistently done, on the choice between residential and domiciliary care. It is a fair guess that the elderly and the disabled will stay out of residences, if they can. Thus, offered community care as an option, the assumption is that they will take it. As this is the choice the government wants anyway, it seems to risk nothing in affirming the right to choose.

However, much depends on how much home help, or whatever, is available (which depends in turn on the level of new funding) and on whether community care is appropriate. Consumers may have their own opinions about what kind of care is appropriate, as the BBC programme 'Getting Rid of Granny' surely made clear. So there *will* be some who choose residential (not to mention hospital) care. There are likely as well to be differences of opinion about which kind of community care is wanted or needed, and in what measure. Will the care manager accept the client's choice or bargain? It is doubtful.

It has been noted that reconstruction of care programming was undertaken in large measure because of the high cost of the so-called perverse incentive. Yet, ironically, the new programme introduces a 'reverse perverse' incentive, rewarding local authorities financially for placing people in private residential care and penalising the local authorities if they provide such care themselves (11). One observes that here is at least one option that the government seeks to close down.

Perhaps a way to visualise the issue of choice in 'virtuality' is to quote from the findings of a study among elderly people in three representative local authorities:

> *The reality is that ... most of those interviewed had no choice in what went into their packet of services ... They certainly had no choice about the time at which the service was delivered, the person who delivered it, or how much they received. ... Rationing was the order of the day. Services were generally acknowledged to be in very short supply, access to them was usually controlled by professional gate keepers ...* (12)

In the same study, social workers earnestly trying to promote participation of elderly people in decisions about their care, conceded that "their assessment of what was needed was dominated by what could be provided, and they tailored the ... information they gave ... to this assessment".

There will be some who choose residential care

'Cognitive dissonance'

Will full implementation of community care alter this pattern? The study comments: "It seems clear that one of the effects of the introduction of assessment for all people seeking residential care and requiring a contribution from public funds ... will be a reduction in the numbers and proportion of elderly people actually exercising choice" (p.312). The study report observes more generally: "There was every indication in this research that a needs-led model of care provision for elderly people ... will prove very difficult to operate without additional resources..."(pp3-4).

In short, people who have had a choice will continue to choose. People who have not, will not. For neither will the situation have changed, except possibly in two ways: contracting-out and encouragement of voluntary organisations would expand choice for care managers and through them conceivably for clients, *if funding were provided and if successful*. On the other hand, the move to care management and devolution of budgets is likely, if anything, to *increase* control over what the client can do. This is its administrative purpose, after all. The government may judge that it has increased choice, but the client who deals with PSS will feel more manipulated than at present.

At one point, social workers declined to undertake assessment for the Social Fund because such a role was deemed incompatible with professional tasks and values (**13**). The British Medical Association takes the position with respect to community care that "it would be inappropriate for the patient's own [General Practitioner] to act as assessor on behalf of the local authority as this might undermine the trust that exists between patients and doctors" (**14**). With care management and budget devolution, social workers will have to judge whether they are engaging in manipulation for the purpose of rationing and whether this is ethical.

User choice in the Children Act

In the background of the Children Act is a difficult struggle over the role of social workers with respect to children and their families. The early inclination of the workers was to support parents in taking care of children. Protecting children against abuse was not the main task; parents were to be helped in a counselling, supportive, and partnership relationship.

This changed over the years as child abuse seized public attention and assumed prominence in caseloads. In recent years, outrageous instances of child abuse have come to public attention, and workers have been criticised "for not being sufficiently quick and firm in their interventions to protect children" (**15**). More or less simultaneously, however, they have been charged with being arbitrary and acting in ways that were "often hasty and ill-planned". Researchers reported parents' complaints that, in taking children into care or indeed in declining to take children into care, social workers failed to give due weight and respect to the parents' judgement.

There has now been professional dispute about these issues for some years. Most social workers have been trained to work in partnership with the members of a child's family. (Obviously, the capacity to do this is affected by caseloads and a degree of anxiety about administrative and community reaction if something goes wrong.) Others think social workers should confine themselves to "the functions required ... by their employing agency

Care management is likely to increase control over clients

The personal social services

operating within a statutory framework". Child protection is seen as the central task, requiring a local authority *to care for* children and not merely to provide social workers who may help (**16**). In a nutshell, the social worker is responsible and has authority.

Lorraine Fox Harding summarised the swings as follows:

> [The 1960s in England and Wales were the] prevention decade when social work practice favoured supporting the natural family and minimising time in care, and the 1970s were the time of child protection spurred on by concern about child abuse ... The 1980s in England and Wales were ... a time of polarisation, of contrasts, and of greater tensions and conflicts in child care policy. (**17**)

In a broad resolution of such issues that is generally acknowledged to be careful and thoughtful, the Children Act sets a higher threshold for local authority intervention in a family and "promotes a notion of partnership between families with children in need and the service providers". Partnership between parents and local authorities is to be encouraged. "The latter, stripped of their powers to assume parental rights ... must work on the basis of negotiation and voluntary agreement." (**18**)

There are problems with operating in this way. Don Staines of the National Society for the Prevention of Cruelty to Children put the problem that he sees like this:

> The reality of dysfunctional families isn't going to go away [because of the Children Act] ... and ultimately practitioners will reframe what is in the Act ... to continue to protect children who need to be protected. (**19**)

Possibly Staines alludes to the fact that the Children Act, while it emphasises partnership, provides the PSS, with court support, with more sanctions and orders than before — in particular, an assessment order which gives social work access to a family for a limited period of time. "There is now a simultaneous emphasis," writes Margaret Adcock, "on partnership with parents, support to families, *with strong protection* to children with minimum reliance on court orders." (emphasis supplied) (**20**).

Another problem is that there have been an average of two inquiries a year since 1974, and there is no reason to suppose that incidents and ensuing public fury will now end. Families do not divide themselves neatly into those which may be worked with and those which will blow up in one fashion or another. Child and family workers working in partnership with parents will, from time to time, unfortunately find that things have gone very wrong. If the principle of partnership with parents is to survive, the public and the media will have to be met with great firmness.

Even more complex as a dilemma is the way the class nature of child and family services works out in terms of partnership. As a rule of thumb one may think of the parties in these services, in ascending order, as (1) a poor or lower working-class client family, (2) a working-class foster family, and (3) a middle-class social worker or other professional. We have already alluded to what happens in this relationship. As Biggs observed about community care, the

The Children Act emphasises partnership but allows more sanctions and orders

'Cognitive dissonance'

parties to this partnership do not meet as equals.

The social class frame of child care is not addressed in the British professional literature that I have seen (**21**), so I ought to declare that in my next observations I am relying on conversations with child and family workers.

What the parents or the mother most fear when a social service department initiates contact is loss of their child. The social worker may know that this is now more difficult to bring about than earlier, but the parent is not likely to feel comfortable about this. So, unless very disturbed indeed, the parent tries to be what the social worker is thought to expect in a person with her status, that is, attentive, accommodating, and polite. She wants the social worker to approve of her and think that she is a fit mother.

If matters come to a case conference, the mother or the parents are likely to be faced with a social worker, a policeman, a health visitor maybe, a physician now and then. In short, the parents are overwhelmed. Much depends on how the chairperson conducts the meeting, to be sure, and the parents are entitled to be accompanied by an advocate. Still, parents are so far rarely 'partners' in these conferences, in any exact sense, and only 'a smallish minority' really 'participate' (**22**). Social workers tell me that they rarely emerge from such a meeting having had their minds changed about what must be done.

If removal is at issue, they must have parental agreement or go to court. Even if they find they must go to court, courts will generally support the social service department — a fact much in the mind of parents throughout the process. And a protection plan, if it does not involve removal, need not in the end have the parents' consent (**23**).

Many decisions do not get into a formal conference. For example, if a mother's partner is accused of child abuse, should he be required or 'helped' to leave the home? (The Children Act now makes provision to help him leave.) In dealing with such a decision, the mother and partner face the social worker, and possibly other professionals as well, alone. Perhaps most telling was the uniform surprise when I queried social workers about whether all parties should be consulted. Those I talked to do not feel that there is any doubt in these matters. Indeed, they tend to be firm in their view that the child is their central concern and, in the end, they know what must be done. So all that went before may have been conversation, but it was not partnership.

About these dilemmas, Jo Tunnard and Mary Ryan observe:

> *Partnership is not about equal power, but about people working together towards a common goal. It is about empowerment, about families having sufficient information to be able to understand and contribute to planning, and having some power to influence the outcome.* (**24**)

It is customary, in talking about the changes that are being made in the personal social services, to say that a culture change is needed. *If Britain is serious about partnership in children's services, a subtle and deep-seated change is required in the way social workers view their clients*. It was noted above that the 1960s was a time of prevention and partnership. I make bold to guess now that that partnership was shaped by

How social workers view clients requires subtle and deep-seated change

27

The personal social services

the same class relationship and was, more exactly, paternalistic (25).

I do not make this argument in order to recommend a culture change. In fact, the degree of commitment and the competence of the workers I have seen is impressive and they are carrying a responsibility to protect children that is laid on them by society. The Children Act gives them strong and discordant signals. For the moment, the protection signal is discreetly delivered but it will come alive with the next scandal, as the professionals understand very well.

The social work profession has to come to terms with the relationship between the authority that PSS inevitably have and the partnership that is now urgently prescribed. The news media will never do this, nor can central government be expected to do it. It is, in the end, a professional matter. How child and family workers behave has to be in accord with what they say and what the law says, or vice versa, or there will be no clarity about their role — and no conviction in defending PSS against the next episode of public outrage.

User choice, concluding comment

Community care and the Children Act arise from distinct and different impulses. The drive to user participation, though it may seem to bridge both programmes in focusing on family responsibility, rises more organically from the family-centered tenor of the Children Act. As for community care, we shall in a moment question whether its effect will be salutary for the family.

Whatever the similarities or differences, in both programmes 'dissonance' in the provisions for user participation arise from a failure to deal with and possibly even to recognise unequal power. One may say that power *must* be unequal, in one case to govern expenditure and in the other case to protect children; and the object is at least to promote more sensitivity to what users say and want. This is fair enough, but the rhetoric ought to be consistent with the reality. If the conclusion is that choice must be qualified, to what extent and in what circumstances should be clear.

This may seem to ask for an unaccustomed restraint and candour in government, not to mention unaccustomed professional clarity, but it is important for the PSS in a particular way. Staff need to be clear about what they are doing. They cannot tacitly mislead themselves and their users without contaminating the relationship between them. This relationship lies at the heart of the work they do.

The family

As with choice, one may mean very different things in espousing families and their rights and responsibilities. The Conservative government has been consistent and explicit that it seeks to change the balance of dependency between families and the government. In the view of recent officials, governments have been doing more and families less. The Conservative government has sought to turn this around. Then, in the Children Act, the government has "leaned against" state intrusion into the family and against paternalism (26). The new messages are clear.

We have already noted the economic environment of families, including the government policies, that lead to crowding together people who would not wish it, youths leaving home prematurely, and demoralisation

> 'User participation' fails to deal with the issue of unequal power

'Cognitive dissonance'

of unemployed adults. Reflection on this leads one to a different definition of family support, having to do with child-rearing, family stability, and the quality of family life.

The cognitive difficulty in administering the PSS is that their objectives, implicit if not always explicit, lie very heavily with the second definition. They are to be attentive to the wishes of their users; and their users, old and young, able and disabled, care very much about the quality of their family life. They are to protect children, and this involves providing them with a stable family, relatively free of strain, in which to grow up.

It cannot be said that social service departments have, in the past, engaged parents on behalf of their children as powerfully as one might wish. A Department of Health review observes that: "Our long-standing traditions of child rescue have meant that ... social service departments have tended to marginalise parents even when acting benevolently towards them." (27)

That is, the focus of a child and family worker on the need of or risk to a child, tends to take all the time that the worker has. Moreover, unless the very greatest pains are taken, the dynamics that follow on taking a child into care lead parents to appear neglectful, if not actually to be so. Workers may be inclined to forget if not actually to dismiss the parents. Grandparents do not even have their names recorded. (28)

We note that, in the reorganisation of social service departments now under way, children's services are being separated from services for elderly and other adults. This is a development that was possibly not anticipated and even not wanted by the government (29). Evidently, the reasons for reorganising in this way include the complexity of each type of service, so that staff cannot be expected to understand both thoroughly; and, second if not first, a desire to protect staff and resources for elderly people against the urgent demands of children. It is widely thought that, because of concern about child abuse, elderly people have increasingly lost out to children. However, if elderly people are to have more, children will have less.

There is already concern that workers do not have enough time. Unallocated cases on the child protection register have increased, in Inner London in particular but in outer London and in the shires as well (30). If reorganisation limits the staffing of children's services (and, of course, *total* PSS resources are relevant too) it can safely be predicted that the drive of the Children Act to engage parents with their children will not be realised. Workers will attend first to the most urgent needs of children, and will not have time for more. Child and family workers are inclined to be child- rather than parent-centered anyway. If they are to broaden their approach they will have to be given more, not less time.

Organisational fission has a second effect that operates against family support. If some workers deal with children and others with elderly people and, possibly, still others with the disabled and learning handicapped, who will serve people who do not fall into these categories? To whom, voluntary organisations have asked, will parents of disabled children older than 19 go for help? What of a couple with a marital problem? Marital problems readily lead to problems about the care of children, so what of prevention? Is prevention — a duty now more broadly laid upon local

There is already concern that workers do not have enough time

The personal social services

authorities than in the Child Care Act of 1980 — to lead PSS to provide services for these other classes of people?

It does not seem likely. Historically, far fewer resources have gone into prevention than protection (**31**). If the organisational structure moves away from people not defined as already having a categorical problem, prevention is even less likely to be done.

For elderly and disabled people, as care managers put pressure on family members to provide more care than they already are, there will also be difficulty. Typically, home care now provided for a disabled person involves perhaps four to six hours a week of home help, meals on wheels and support from a district nurse (**32**). Home care for elderly people is even more modest (**33**). The White Paper and guidance specify that priority should be given to those with the greatest need (**34**). These are people who will need very intensive packages of care, indeed. This suggests that those who now receive typical packages or even less will find them harder to come by, particularly as general hospitals press on with their policy of earlier discharge and psychiatric hospitals turn out patients (**35**).

The 'most in need' policy (**36**) appears to be aimed at maximum savings of money, though even in these terms it may not entirely have been thought through (see section 7). In any event, when the modest packages of care are withdrawn or not available, family members who can, so to speak, share care with social services will find that they must provide all the care. Instead of the reprieve that many need, the evidence is, they will be burdened further. It does not seem likely that this will be sound for families, nor is it even clear that it will reduce dependency. The truth is, one does not know; with respect to families, at any rate, it is a leap into the dark.

We do understand something about the broad effect of these pressures. Young people may be induced to "lose touch" with their elders (**37**). The elderly are likely to go without care rather than rely on family members, who are hard-pressed in other ways. We have seen that carers may themselves be very young or elderly, ill, and distracted by pressures of all sorts. As they provide care, or even more care — because many of them will, if they must — their husbands and children will also feel the burden.

It seems fair to observe that the direction in which PSS are moving to implement the Children Act and community care would integrate services around individuals and fragment services to families. Prevention will decline further — because the specialised organisational structure will lead to overlooking it and because the 'most in need' policy and an unavoidable tendency to deal first with children at risk will target those with the greatest or most complex needs.

The PSS workers who try to deal with this have been trained to think about all this from the point of view of the whole family. Pressure on them, or indeed a requirement on them, to practise otherwise will tend to break down their professionalism.

Concluding comment

Many issues are unresolved in how PSS will administer the Children Act and community care. Everyone understands this; such complex changes require time to work out. How will care management be administered, and is it workable? Will it lead to economies or not; will

Far fewer resources go into prevention than protection

'Cognitive dissonance'

it lead to better quality care? Will voluntary and for-profit organisations come in to offer the variety of services that are hoped for, and will inspection assure quality? And so forth.

However, some issues seem to build chronic dissonance into PSS programming. User choice is one such issue, butting against the power of social service workers to allocate funds, on the one hand, and to make judgements about what children require, on the other. Another such issue is professionalism's foundation in thinking of the family as a whole. Administration of the new programmes appears to shape itself in a manner that is at odds with this way of thinking.

Choice and the family are not peripheral issues. They go to the heart of professional practice. If workers are required to behave one way and to believe they are thinking another way, they will find techniques for reducing discomfort. There will be a growth in cynicism, in anti-professionalism, and an inclination to define their jobs privately while avoiding accountability. It would seem important to avoid these outcomes.

6 The Children Act and child abuse

Registered child abuse is not likely soon to decline

It would be unwise to think about the Children Act and the social service departments without grasping the centrality of child abuse to local authority planning. First, I offer the briefest historical comment mainly to underline a single point: reported child abuse will not diminish and may indeed increase.

Child abuse was recognised as a problem in the 1960s, first by physicians (as in the United States) and then by the National Society for the Prevention of Cruelty to Children (**1**). It burst upon public consciousness with the Maria Colwell case, since when instances of child abuse — particularly sexual abuse of children — have not failed to rouse public passion. The rate of children registered as abused doubled between 1983 and 1987 (**2**), and currently child protection referrals are increasing by around 20 per cent each year (**3**). However, public inquiries and professionals tend to be (rightly) sceptical whether such figures reflect an actual increase in abuse (**4**).

Within the past hundred years, children were treated far worse than now. People led what today we would regard as brutish lives. Many did not have private beds, let alone private bedrooms. Children were *property;* the very idea of childhood had only recently been invented. One may see in medieval paintings, for example, that children were represented as diminutive adults. The report on Cleveland notes that, in Paris in the 1860s, Tardieu "wrote at length on rape, incest and anal interference of young children" (**5**). Youths were sent to work in other people's homes as domestics — one-third of all French girls during the nineteenth century, for example. For many, service was a channel to degradation, destitution, and often prostitution (**6**). In Britain, the Punishment of Incest Act of 1908 was a response to rising concern about the treatment of children (**7**).

In the course of western society's comparatively recent 'civilising process', having to do with behaviour at the table, blowing one's nose, behaviour in the bedroom, wearing underwear, and so forth, children were generally regarded as natural forces requiring to be tamed. The view that education is an exercise in breaking the child's spirit justifies emotional and physical abuse and reaches into our own times. Recent examples are the 'pin-down' child abuse scandals and the children's home director convicted of child abuse whose philosophy was "to break children before caring for them" (**8**).

Historically speaking, then, civility is a thin veneer, especially as it addresses children. What makes child abuse prominent now is probably not that children are being treated worse, but that how badly we treat them is surfacing and being defined as unacceptable.

As Barbara Nelson observed in a book that tried to grasp why child abuse became an issue in the United States just when it did, it was linked to a general assertion of civil rights (**9**). Similarly, the present reaction against child abuse is one among a number of moves taking a stand against abuse and violence — by women addressing men, by men and women talking about children, by a society seized with the idea that brutality must be replaced with civility. If this is so, deep re-education will take time and *we will not for some time see a decline in registered child abuse.*

Unfortunately, when child abuse came to public attention it was defined in terms of a so-called medical model — a distinguishable pathological agent attacking an individual or

The Children Act and child abuse

family that could be treated in a prescribed manner and would disappear (**10**). Actually, none of this characterises child abuse. It is rather "the nature of British society that makes it possible for children to be abused" — its type of intimate domestic organisation, the value placed upon privacy, the power that adults have over children (**11**). Values that tolerate physical disciplining of children make their contribution; so, too, do poverty and deprivation. These are qualities that are not readily influenced nor, for some of these values at least, would there would be much inclination to change.

With the medical model in mind, one would expect that abusers can be treated and will improve, and in time child abuse will be controlled like any infectious disease. When social service departments patently fail to bring this about, the natural reaction is anger at the social workers. It may be that social workers have contributed to this misunderstanding, giving the impression that if there were more of them or they were more specialised, child abuse would be reduced (**12**).

The truth is that social workers and other helping professionals cannot do this, any more than the contribution of psychiatrists to the treatment of mental illness can greatly reduce its prevalence. Very few professionals are well enough trained to treat child abusers, and the success rate is not high. Nor does treatment of an abuser prevent abuse elsewhere (**13**). None of this says that treatment and control should not be provided — of course, they should, but only that moderating child abuse is a very long-range effort.

The centrality of child abuse to planning for the Children Act lies in its capacity to overwhelm children's services and the overall mission of social service departments, separation of functions notwithstanding. There is no way a department can fail to respond to the threat of serious harm to a child, nor will councillors or the public tolerate failure to respond. An early effect of a swelling child abuse caseload is to reduce and eventually wipe out work with parents and preventive work. This sequence can be observed in the recent history of American child welfare agencies.

Another danger of failing to think through a position about child abuse is that child and family workers will be more inclined to seek to take children into care. This comes to seem safer for the child and leaves no possibility that the social worker will be blamed when something goes wrong. In fact, the number of children taken into care — which had been falling for some years until 1985 — rose sharply in 1986 and 1987, following the death of Jasmine Beckford. In subsequent years, the numbers fell again (**14**).

It is important to understand that taking a child into care can be its own form of abuse. Research shows "that periods in public care have further impaired the life chances of some children and young people" (**15**) The work load implications of child abuse have to be faced. Thought has to be given to educating the public to understand the historical and current social context of child abuse, to the difficult and inevitably fallible judgements that professionals must make, and to what can and cannot reasonably be expected of social service departments. The Cleveland report recognised and stated this need:

Moderating child abuse is a very long-range effort

The personal social services

We are ... concerned about the extent of misplaced adverse criticism social workers have received from the media and elsewhere. There is a danger that social workers ... will be demoralised. Some may hesitate to do what is right. Social workers need the support of the public to continue in the job the public needs them to do. It is time the public and the press gave it to them. **(16)**

Even so and at best, child abuse will present a considerable problem in maintaining balanced PSS programming.

Cost-effectiveness, assessment and care management in community care

Cost-effectiveness and assessment

Members of the government have from time to time said explicitly that the drive for community care does not reflect a conviction that it will be cheaper (**1**). However, a subtext of policy statements and guidance, on cost-effectiveness in particular, appears to represent just such a belief; in any case, it is widely held. It may therefore be useful to indicate why it is not so.

In order to be concise in the material that follows, I contrast residential and community care *as generalisations*. However, the two terms and their costs are really different for different groups of people. For elderly people, community care has tended to mean keeping them at home. For people with learning disabilities or mental illness, it has meant de-institutionalisation. The former may be less expensive, though expensive. The latter is likely to be very expensive, indeed (**2**).

I offer five reasons why community care in general does not produce savings. First, elderly and disabled people do not want residential care (**3**), and their carers "conduct a private, unheralded guerilla war against the force of provider incentives" (**4**). So, despite difficulties, people manage to stay at home, accounting for the evidence that not very many who are actually in residences could manage at home. There have been contrary findings (**5**) but they are not weighty. In short, elderly and disabled people screen themselves out of residential care, perhaps more severely than is desirable, and leave little for policy to contribute.

General reluctance to enter residences suggests a second point: professional assessment, when requested or required, may lead to a recommendation to enter a residence or an even more expensive treatment facility (**6**). Obviously, the effect in such cases is to *raise* the cost of care.

Third, we have noted the government's intention to concentrate community services on those who are most in need, that is, those who may be diverted from residential care. If only cost is considered, this is arguably logical. However, disabled people in particular may require "intensive packages [which] can involve 24-hour attendance with a great deal of personal help with getting up and going to bed, washing, dressing, toileting, and eating" (**7**). It may be doubtful that many PSS will get involved in such intensive provision, but those that do will find costs raised rather than lowered (**8**).

More generally, the level of community care across the country is "patchy" (**9**). Indeed, the reallocation of care resources from *all others* would not be sufficient to care for those who are defined as high priority (**10**). Thus, care would have to be enriched considerably, at some cost, if people are to be maintained at home who might otherwise enter institutions.

Fourth, this potential cost is compounded by the so-called 'Pandora effect'. That is, expansion of home-based services would lead to expanded demand for them (**11**). One can readily see this: your neighbour, who is not more frail, gets a package of services which you have been managing without for several years, albeit with difficulty. If such services are now available, shouldn't you have them too?

In other words, home-based services cannot be ladled out onto islands of users that suit the government's objectives, leaving large lacunae between. This would not be a design for citizen satisfaction. Carers and the people they are

The level of community care across the country is 'patchy'

The personal social services

caring for are operating under great stress, as we have seen, so levelling out between the islands would involve great cost.

Fifth and finally, in Section 2 we discussed the possibilities that family, friends, or neighbours would provide care at little or no cost to the government. To sum up that part of Section 2 in six words: it is not at all likely. Philip Abrams, who had been working on the matter long and intensively, used three sentences:

Community care is not likely to save government money

> Governments have been pushing what they call the informal system of care, and they have got it wrong. They will need to spend money to provide back-up services. If we want to go into neighbourhood care in a big way in urban areas, the evidence [is that] we cannot rely on volunteer housewives who simply don't have time or sufficient numbers to do the work. (**12**)

The issues here are not new, of course. Monroe County in New York State has conducted a long series of projects doing multidisciplinary evaluation of the elderly, with a view to reducing the number in institutions. As early as twenty years ago, they reported improved quality of life for their patients but no reduction in cost or rate of institutionalisation (**13**). They report much the same reasons as are offered above.

Much of the optimism that is abroad about ultimate savings from a policy of community care rests on the reports of experimental projects such as in Kent, Darlington, and Gateshead (**14**). One has to bear in mind that such projects have had an investment of services, interest and research funding that is not likely to persist in normal operations. Further, painstaking review of the research methods casts question on the broad applicability of their findings (**15**).

Perhaps most persuasive on this point, however, is the progressive disenchantment of Bleddyn Davies, who was at one time the strongest advocate of savings through community care, assessment and care management. Davies' writing style tends to be dense, if enlivened by flashes of metaphor and allegory, and it is possible that the moderation in his enthusiasm has escaped general notice. By 1989, he was writing of the difficulties of improving "marginal productivity" and "targeting" in the projects, and the necessity of:

> a high ratio of investment to expenditure on direct production of services and with it the management and organisational activities associated with an industry with a high rate of technical progress operating in a turbulent environment. (**16**)

In 1991, he wrote that more services would not necessarily save money, that efficiency and targeting in the experimental projects are poor and hard to improve, and that resources would have to be found for increased spending on investment if community care is to be made to work — an eventual outcome about which he sounded hopeful but far from certain (**17**). Thus, community care is not likely to offer savings in government money, not in the short run as indicated earlier and not in the long run.

After all this, it may be useful to offer a reminder that there are reasons why community care *is* sound policy — because

Cost-effectiveness, assessment and care management in community care

people want it, because it provides "higher morale, decreased loneliness, improved health, increased mobility, reduced dependence, increased social contact and increased capacity to cope" (**18**). The economy of this statement should not cloud its importance.

As we have now moved on to other qualities than cost and efficiency, perhaps it is appropriate to question the policy of giving priority in community care to those whose "needs are greatest" (**19**). I do not want to argue that two or three hours of care a week for people whose lives will be eased is more important than gathering the care hours together for far fewer but far needier people. But neither is it clear that the greatest-need policy is sound. It may well be that small investments of care at an early point will prevent physical and mental deterioration and avoid larger needs for care later.

Peter Gorbach put the point like this:

> *... to target resources to those at risk of admission to residential care and also to those whose health and social functioning may decline if they do not receive help can give rise to conflicting priorities. With limited resources and large numbers of elderly people requiring a variety of types of home care, a short-term focus on preventing admission could have long-term consequences for ... others.* (**20**)

How does it come about that this greatest need policy, affecting many thousands of people, was put forward on grounds of presumed saving of money without any attention or debate at all about its equity or morality or about public priorities? Because, after all, no one thinks that elected councillors will pluck two or three hours a week of meals on wheels or home help away from hundreds of constituents?

Care management

Care management (synonymous with case management, in the discussion here) derives from work in the United States over many years. It is a method of dealing with the fragmentation of services, intending in principle to co-ordinate them for each individual client. It was conceived earliest in Welfare (or Social Service or Human Service) Departments, which have suffered from fragmentation for many years now, and was adopted more recently by health insurance companies. The latter may be interested in bringing services together, but are far more interested in using managed care, as they call it, for cost control.

I do not address care management by insurance companies; it is heatedly controversial, particularly with physicians who resent lay control over their treatment plans. However, its sources and uses are somewhat different from the British government's, which is interested in cost control, to be sure, but seems genuinely to seek to improve care. Moreover, in any locality in Britain there is likely to be one major purchaser - the local authority. With respect to health care in the United States, in any locality there may be hundreds of purchasers, each doing managed care — often several care managers for one patient.

With respect to British personal social services, there is some uncertainty about what care management is intended to cover. This uncertainty begins with the White Paper, *Caring for People*. "The Government sees considerable merit," it says, "in nominating a 'case manager'

Early, small investments of care may avoid larger needs later

The personal social services

to take responsibility for ensuring that individuals' needs are regularly reviewed, resources are managed effectively and that each service user has a single point of contact" (3.3.2). Not much more than a hundred words further along, it speaks of care management as identifying people in need and planning and securing delivery of care (3.3.4).

For this reason I decline to distinguish care from case management: if there is a distinction, it is that case management is what a social worker or other professional does with a client or claimant (the former White Paper language cited) and care management covers administrative procedures (the latter language) (**21**). Obviously, the White Paper covers both with one term; in the field also, the two meanings are folded together. The White Paper called them both case management; lately, care management seems to be preferred.

American social service application of the term, care management, is very broad indeed — all the way from a very specialised and sophisticated service for very disabled or disturbed clients (**22**) to a highly practical service directed at public assistance recipients who are required to train for or find paid work (**23**). Close to what is intended in Britain is the State of Wisconsin experience, where nursing home construction was halted and money already allocated for it turned over to community agencies, which were charged with developing community care and care management (**24**).

It is difficult to generalise from current American literature. An overwhelming proportion of journal articles are written to report success, but a variety of disincentives inhibit reporting failure — in the United States, at any rate. It is my impression that failure of care management is epidemic in Departments of Human Services — for lack of adequate funding, to begin with, so that one never gets to the question of whether the concept is sound. The Wisconsin experience reported success — dependably, it seemed. Yet, even as the report was written Wisconsin was entering a period of financial stringency and the article expressed anxiety about its effect on the experimental programme (**25**).

Reviewing the American literature on care management over the last fifteen years, James J. Callahan concluded:

Fifteen years of research on community-based care management fails to support most of the claims of its effectiveness in solving the problems for which it was intended. (**26**)

Asking why, then, care management is supported for elderly people in particular, he thought that the argument is that they want it and need it to get access to myriad services. But "older persons," he writes, "do not want case management and are certainly not willing to pay for it". Nor are they, in general, less likely than anyone else to be able to manage their own affairs. What they want is personal social services, and these should be expanded.

If one thinks that care management means a named person to organise assessment, co-ordination, and continuous overseeing of an individual's care, questions arise. For example, a good deal of what clients ask is simple and straightforward (a pair of crutches, for example). It would be frustrating and cost more to name a care manager than simply to authorise provision. So there has to be some way to sort

Failure of care management is epidemic in the States

Cost-effectiveness, assessment and care management in community care

out who is to be dealt with one way and who another. Government guidance lays responsibility for working this out on local authorities, and it is being worked on.

Another question is whether the care manager acts as a PC at a street corner directing traffic, or a skilled therapist able to deal with anxieties and feelings associated with ageing and disability. The British Association of Social Workers opts for the latter and, indeed, believes that all care managers should be qualified social workers (**27**). This raises problems of resource and staffing, not to mention inter-professional issues. This, too, can be sorted out by establishing a screening procedure; not everyone needs to be listened to and understood, and some people resent being led into a discussion when they are seeking a simple outcome.

However, one must wonder whether in the end arrangements will be much different. In general, the practice has been to decide at a client's initial approach whether a simple one-time (or two- or three-time) transaction is advisable, or a more complicated assessment or a package of care and continuing review. The matter has then been disposed of or appropriately assigned. Now, this is all to be made more formal. More formality might, indeed, assure packaging or continuity in situations in which the need for them has been overlooked. On the other hand, if care management is truly to mean a change, staff will be given new titles, trained in techniques of budget management and contract negotiation, and perhaps given devolved budgets. One must be concerned that this will introduce a new stratum of practice, compounding staff and organisational interconnections that need to be made on behalf of a particular client or plan.

This implies delay, if not failure, in providing services. Linda Challis put it as follows:

> ... *The history of co-ordination at both a service and a case level has not been encouraging... It has proved a rather weak and unreliable instrument to overcome organisational and professional rigidities. There seems little reason to suppose that case management will do any better; [analysis] may suggest that it will do rather less well.* (**28**)

All this has cost implications. In long-term care projects in the United States, care management costs have ranged from $96 to $134 a month, and private care management services charge an average of $50 an hour plus expenses (**29**).

In a bureaucracy (a term I do not intend pejoratively) hierarchy tends to proliferate, and there is some indication that the care management systems now being devised will not lodge responsibility for a care plan in one person, but will rather create new overseers of how money is allocated (**30**). There may be devolution of budgets, but in many cases to a 'team leader', or someone higher up — not to the line worker. There will almost certainly be better accounting for money or, at any rate, *more* accounting for money, but it is far from certain that there will be more or better community care. If there are more people to check with or get approval from, care may be worse.

Closing comment

In the implementation of community care, PSS are making a number of assumptions that are dubious, at best. Community care is not in any way likely to be self-financing. If central

In the end, will arrangements be much different?

The personal social services

government or local authorities do not provide the additional funds that are needed, they will not be provided. At one point, local authorities said as much to the then Secretary of State for Health, and he announced a phased timetable to allow them to improve their administration of the programme (**31**). This is not the issue. Improved administration can make better use of funds; it cannot substitute for funds.

Care management is not a panacea. Support for it is derived from a view of American experience which must have focused on some very special places and moments. The experimental projects in Britain that are cited in support of care management also took place in very special circumstances with special investments of money and interest. At the heart of the problem of care management is that it cannot, like reconstituted DNA, be inserted into a chaotic structure and organise it. It needs an orderly and hospitable administrative structure; in present circumstances, few PSS provide this. Moreover, as Bleddyn Davies has now tried several times to say, in order to work it requires not less money but more money, much more money.

Such assumptions and interesting ideas, many of them untested at best, together with other ideas like the purchaser-provider split are to be introduced into the PSS at the same time, and without necessary funding. The financial situation will quite distort these administrative devices. Assessment and care management, never entirely removed from rationing, will be used *primarily* for rationing. Thus, they will lose credibility with users, who were supposed to be partners, and with the staff, who may worry about ethics and playing straight with clients. If care management and assessment might be productive in providing community care, this will not be demonstrated in this way of approaching it.

A final observation before concluding: it has been observed, by Age Concern for one, that the government is "moving the goalposts" (**32**). That is, long-term care that was available in the health sector is now being moved over to the private and voluntary sectors. This means that a physician who decided that a patient could be discharged from hospital once faced the responsibility (or his service faced the responsibility) to see that other care would be provided. Now the physician and Health Service are discharged from this constraint. If patients' families cannot, PSS must deal with this issue in whatever numbers the Health Service lays upon them. NHS and the Department of Health may require that co-ordination be established (**33**), but each service will answer to its own imperatives.

Community care is a sound idea from the point of view of the people who might use it, and has been for all the years it has been talked about. It would be useful and exciting to stimulate its provision. Somewhere in the higher reaches of government, judgements have to be made about how much expansion is feasible and an attempt made to do this. The rhetoric ought to be adjusted to the resources, and the management system thought through in relation to the scale that is intended. From all indications (**34**), PSS may need not more but less — and perhaps better — administration.

Care management cannot be inserted into a chaotic structure to organise it

Brinksmanship in administration

A cautionary tale

I begin with a cautionary tale about public child welfare in the United States.

Prior to the 1960s, the ideology of child welfare was clear: a family-centred service, classless, with well-trained professionals, not directed at financial issues. In principle, financial issues were dealt with by the government in other ways. To be sure, the achievement fell far short of the goal, but the programme operated reasonably well and the leaders of the field knew where they were trying to go.

From the 1960s on, child welfare suffered a series of blows that left the programme in a shambles. For a variety of reasons, citizen interest in children's issues diminished. The employment standard to which local child welfare agencies had been held (line workers with a graduate degree in social work) was abandoned. Employment standards declined for other reasons too and, at higher levels, specialisation in management took precedence over professional social work.

Next, particular family developments from 1960 on — more single parent families and more prevalent substance abuse, for example — added to child welfare's caseload. Real family income started a steady decline in 1973, particularly among poorer families. The real income of the poorest fifth of the population dropped one-third in fifteen years. Lately, as many as 40 per cent of children in substitute care have come from families receiving welfare.

From one perspective, another blow to child welfare in 1963 was the identification of child abuse as a specific family problem, analogous to a physical illness (see Section 6 for more on this point). This led to public dissatisfaction with child welfare agencies, and an enormous volume of new cases.

By the 1970s, researchers had documented widespread, unfortunate outcomes for children placed in foster family homes. Many stayed in substitute care indefinitely, becoming increasingly disturbed as they moved from home to home. After a while, *Beyond the Best Interests of the Child* staked out the premise that child welfare workers were too indecisive, failing to sever children's ties to pathological parents so they could be adopted by proper, loving parents (**1**). In the professional controversy that followed, it seemed as if the interests of parents and children were opposed to each other. This reinforced a growing professional inclination, sparked by public indignation, to separate children from their natural parents.

Coming around again, by 1980 a movement to clarify and support the family relationships of children gathered strength. Congress passed a bill along these lines in 1981. Unfortunately, the pressures that had been generated had led child welfare agencies to confine their attention to the abused and neglected children who were their clearest statutory mandate. Many agencies no longer had units to deal with children in their own homes nor, if they had such units, staff with the time and skill to do what appeared to be the less urgent tasks of family counselling and support. In fragmented ways, some agencies staged special efforts to achieve the objectives of the legislation, but these did not alter the generally chaotic work that was prevalent by this time.

Public anger at social workers and child welfare agencies reached a high level. Support for all public services was coming to be seriously

In the US, public anger with the PSS led to cutbacks

The personal social services

In America, the question has become how to rescue so debased a system

constrained; public anger at social service departments meant that they were cut back even more than other public services. Thus, they had more to do and less to do it with.

Almost unnoticed, such developments led to the work of line staff members becoming increasingly routine. Child welfare is administered by state and local agencies. Nevertheless, a dissatisfied Congress undertook to legislate the content of their work, state legislatures enacted 24-hour response times and six-month mandatory reviews, guidance descended on local agencies in an ungentle snow and administrators and supervisors became more prescriptive in more and more detail.

Discretion was limited and the line worker's job became increasingly routine and simple-minded — in a word, stultifying. Over the years, the more dedicated and skilful workers drifted away. Workers remained who could not get other jobs or were holding on for approaching retirement. Workers newly taken on were influenced by the poor work attitudes of those who had stayed. One of the most demanding jobs in the personal social services was and is (in general) performed by the least mission-oriented and least skilful workers (2).

As administrative history, the story of American child welfare agencies in the last thirty years may be read as systematic destruction of a functioning organisation. It is almost as if this was done deliberately, but of course it was not. Many of the changes were made for what appeared to be good reasons: entry qualifications for social workers were reduced at a time when so-called 'paraprofessional' workers were seen as having advantages, and anyway not enough workers with graduate degrees were available. *Beyond the Best Interests ...* was intended to sharpen skills and responsibility. Federal legislation in 1981 was adopted to correct an anti-family tendency in child welfare practice. Stronger regulation and oversight would assure that specific responsibilities could not be overlooked. And so on.

Implemented in isolation, some of these measures might have turned out to be sound. Taken together, in rapid sequence and in combination with pressures like child abuse and rising poverty, they created a sense of continual, meaningless change. Skills and responsibility were not sharpened and a more family-oriented practice was not secured. The mission of the agencies was pushed out of mind in the workers' drive to survive each current cutback or change in administration and to satisfy formal requirements (24 hour turn-around on complaints, for example) in a mechanical fashion. In-service training that floated above and apart from actual day-to-day practice came to have little meaning, and new staff members, however promising, would be undermined within weeks.

In the last two or three years, several national commissions have attempted to address these problems without, in my view, being able to arrive at substantial and useful conclusions. The programme has so deteriorated that it is hard to know what to do. Around the country child welfare agencies are being charged in federal court with child neglect, and are losing the cases; but the question has become how to rescue a system that has been so debased.

The Personal Social Services

The point of setting down this outline history may be seen if we review prior sections of this paper.

Brinksmanship in administration

The clients of Britain's PSS are poor people, partly because the qualities that lead to poverty also lead to needing the departments' services and partly because poor people are more vulnerable when departments are inclined to intervene in their affairs. Lack of money is by no means a complete account of their impoverishment. Their family and social resources tend also to be over-strained (see Section 2).

The world outside the PSS holds little promise for improvement. Indeed, the situation seems likely to get worse. Social security has altered in a variety of ways that affects the poor adversely. Of particular relevance here, it leads to increased demand for residential care. The production and availability of housing is constrained, especially for those with low incomes. Work patterns have taken a dangerous turn, with characteristics — low pay, a third of the work force engaged in peripheral work, high unemployment and one million workers unemployed for a year or more — that will not quickly yield to corrective measures. It promises increasing numbers of clients for PSS. Moreover short-falls, as in housing and social security, create virtually insoluble problems that the PSS are nevertheless charged with solving (see Section 3).

One would think — certainly the local authorities think — that trying to cope with such problems requires more staff and more money. They have said that they need £150 million more in 1992-3 just to implement the Children Act (**3**). But it is not planned that more money in serious magnitudes should be provided; in many cases, less is being allowed.

There has been some wishful thinking about the money that might be diverted from residential care of elderly, disabled and mentally ill people and used for increased community care services, but this is a chimera (see Sections 4 and 7). Nor are the poor people who are the PSS clients or their families able to provide the care that the National Health Service declines to provide and PSS find they cannot provide (see Section 2). The funding problem is accentuated for PSS because their clients are not active politically and the staff in direct contact with them are not a politically powerful interest group. In heated competition for money among the local public services, PSS are not likely to do well.

In the last three or four years, two weighty new sets of responsibilities have been laid on the PSS, in the NHS and Community Care Act and the Children Act (see Section 4). The rationale for this legislation is not without ambiguity and difficulties. There is a disturbing paradox, for example, in the Children Act's juxtaposition of partnership with parents and increased statutory power through the courts (see Section 5). Nevertheless, at its core, this legislation seeks objectives that a considerable body of opinion agrees are forward-looking and desirable. How much more confusing, then, that only guidance is provided to help PSS do what is asked. If money flowed as freely as guidance, there would be less problem in moving forward.

A good deal of head and heart work is also laid on staff. If there is to be a culture change, as it is said, professional issues will have to be sorted out with respect to choice, partnership, and user participation (see Section 5). Everyone understands that this involves not only a thought process, but changing habits and yielding vested interests.

If money flowed as freely as guidance, problems would be fewer

The personal social services

These are not easy to achieve; they require professional leadership and a particular organisational context.

There are other changes that have not been discussed in this report — a movement to specialism, the purchaser-provider split, establishing systems for inspection and regulation, fee-charging and a movement to means-testing. Whether sound or not, they create more change for staff to adjust to; and without getting into deeper issues, on the face of it means-testing and inspection and regulation add to administrative burden.

Not to be overlooked is child abuse, an irresistible consumer of time, effort, and services (see Section 6), notwithstanding the effort of PSS to protect services for the elderly by reorganising into specialist teams. Staff time is funnelled into child protection and preventive services decline.

The administrative climate

The personal social services have for some time been characterised by continual reorganisation. In 1968 Richard Titmuss wrote about the rapidity of change as a problem at a time that now seems comparatively pastoral and peaceful and a government study pointed to the problem in 1982 (**4**). There were two major reorganisations in the early 1970s, and subsequent local government reorganisations affecting PSS operations. Apart from these, social service departments "go in for a lot of reorganisation ... major root and branch upheavals". It is not uncommon for some to be reorganising in one direction (decentralising, for example) while simultaneously others are going the other way (centralising) (**5**). And now there appears to be a prospect of sweeping reorganisation of local government. As a result, staff have considerable uncertainty and sense of instability, combined with the deepest scepticism about the purposes of whatever is the current fashion in reorganisation. "SSDs urgently need a stable welfare environment for the demands placed on us," writes Ian White (**6**). Tessa Jowell offers a warning:

> *Our professional world is spinning so fast it is hard to maintain one's bearings and the uncertainties, real or speculative, are in danger of sabotaging competence, creativity, and confidence.* (**7**)

There has been considerable criticism of social workers and the PSS in the media in recent years — for loose overseeing and poor administration, for bureaucratic rigidity, and for incompetence. As a result staff develop a "siege mentality" (**8**). That is, morale is low and staff feel unappreciated or that they have not been given the wherewithal to do their work. They draw together against higher authorities and the public. In the circumstances, it is not surprising that vacancies for social workers are increasing, and turnover is rising. In 1987, local authorities had more severe shortages for social workers than for any other profession and the difficulty was growing (**9**). In the last four years, there has been 60 per cent turnover among directors of social service (**10**).

In accounting for the difficulty in recruiting social workers, the Audit Commission displayed a curious blind spot and illustrated another problem.

> *Many managers [they wrote] — including some in local government — believe that*

Constant reorganisation leads to a 'siege mentality'

Brinksmanship in administration

life would be easier if they did not have to employ professionals. Professionals take years to train; their qualifications, when achieved, enable them to move easily from one employer to another ...; their primary commitment is often to their profession rather than their employer; and they doubt the ability of outsiders to judge the value of their work. ...[They] can create management problems. (**11**)

The Commission offers this observation with some coolness in order to tell local authorities that professionals are important, after all; the work cannot be done without them. Yet, in examining why turnover is high and recruitment difficult (relatively low salaries, expanding need for staff), the Commission does not seem to appreciate the significance of its observation. There appears to be a growing gulf between managers and line workers. Social workers widely complain that, in a shift to administration by general managers, the purposes of their work are being subordinated and they are undervalued. This, too, leads to disaffection and turnover.

All the while caseloads, that is, work for each staff member, have been increasing (**12**). "The effects of shortages are evident both in the provision of inferior services to the public (compared with what had been planned) and in inadequate management and control systems" (**13**). "The overall picture ... is of public services under strain, with only patchy delivery..." (**14**). As a result, legislation is increasingly prescriptive.

There appears to be a growing gulf between managers and line workers

45

9 Conclusion: The declining slope

Does it not seem clear that, while the process is by no means as far advanced, the PSS are embarked on the same declining slope that America's child welfare agencies took? The content is different but the same dynamics are put in place, step by step.

British agencies with rather high morale and doing an arguably creditable job in the 1970s were subjected to one change after another, some changes undoubtedly sound in themselves. Outside forces (poverty, abused children, family breakdown) built up great pressures for the agencies. In many places and at times they failed badly and they were and are criticised.

Managers replaced social workers in many top-ranking positions and ignored or indeed complained about the professionals. When they can find other work, social workers leave. Now they are asked to take on extraordinary new tasks; they doubt that they can be performed under existing conditions. They are asked to pursue objectives that they do not believe the government is serious about; otherwise it would provide resources to achieve them.

In 1985, a panel of inquiry into the circumstances surrounding the death of Jasmine Beckford published their report and recommendations (**1**) and a year later a research team undertook a review of progress. They concluded that little that was constructive had happened because, in the state in which the Social Service Department found itself, the lessons developed by the inquiry were "unlearnable". The Department was so disorganised and demoralised and available resources so far short of what was needed that recommendations could not be implemented (**2**). For example:

... administrative systems are in a very poor state ... there are great variations between areas; the physical fabric of establishments is very serious and so too are the conditions under which staff is working; the staffing of some parts of the Department is at a critical level (3).

That is, the situation no longer lends itself to ready remedy. Brent is only one London borough, after all, but it is a warning.

Challenging a person or an organisation can produce good work, even great work. There is some magnitude of challenge, however, that produces breakdown. It does not take a prophet to read the future, if matters go on like this. Too much work with too little resources, change that cannot be assimilated and seems meaningless, and a sorting-out of staff that increases the proportion who are alienated will produce poor work. This will, in turn, further diminish public support, tending to reduce resources and leave the workers who remain feeling embattled. The time will come when no one knows how to restore these departments to sound functioning.

The situation no longer lends itself to ready remedy

10 Recommendations

The danger, then, is not that the personal social services may fail to perform but that, in failing, they may become so badly disorganised that there is no road back. One Director of Social Services displays a poster in his office advertising a Samuel Beckett play: "No Matter. Try Again. Fail Again. Fail Better." It is a rueful quotation. One has to sympathise but, still, there is no longer a margin for substantial failure.

The personal social services are a £4 billion-plus enterprise, staffed in some large part with skilled and committed workers. They have a vast fund of experience and relationships with their communities. They are the last resort of hundreds of thousands of troubled and disadvantaged residents. They need a reasonable framework in which to do their work. Neither blaming nor exhortation has helped; these are not what is needed.

I offer recommendations in this particular context: I have dwelt on the economic environment — cutbacks in social security, homelessness, and unemployment — in order to be clear about the magnitude of the problem that the PSS face. I will not be addressing this background, however. That would have to emerge from a different kind of study. In any case, I do not feel franchised to propose the expenditure of billions of pounds, as recommendations addressing those issues would surely require.

Second, it is not possible to go back to a previous status quo even if one wanted to. The genie is out of the bottle, in the words of the well worn adage, and the changes in ways of working embodied in the NHS and Community Care Act and the Children Act are the order of the day as, at least in a measure, are the purchaser-provider split and privatisation.

And finally, it must be obvious that I would not recommend still another reorganisation.

My recommendations come in three parts, which may be named restraint, diversion, and resources.

Restraint

A great deal has been laid on the PSS. Some local authorities have greeted the changes with enthusiasm; many have moved dutifully to implement at least some of them; and not a few are resisting changes large and small. Some have done little or nothing about the purchaser-provider split and privatisation; many are treating care management as a change in administrative oversight rather than in practice; and very few are identifying 'children in need' in any meaningful way.

It would be well if the government would look benignly on the local authorities' efforts to adapt to these changes in their own time and in a manner consistent with local capacities and cultures. The effect would be to give the local authorities room and time to absorb the changes, or those of the changes that each wishes to absorb. The effect would also be to provide a test in the UK of the merits of ideas which are, after all, untested or gravely disputed.

In particular, many local authorities are dubious about the merits of giving up the provider role entirely (**1**). It would remove flexibility and an option for them where options may be needed. It would subject users to a variety of dangers in private market provision — the possibility of screening and selection for certain kinds of users, the possibility of vacating particular fields or of

It is not possible to go back to the previous status quo

The personal social services

bankruptcy, the possibility of monopoly provision. Moreover, if it is reasonable that local authority provision needs a yardstick, so too does private provision. It would be well to tolerate diversity in this matter, at least for a time. Among other things, restraint and diversity require correction of the 'reverse perverse' incentive (see Section 5).

With the passage of several years, central government might decide to press more firmly for implementation; this is always open to government. In any event, at present many departments do not have the capacity for meaningful implementation. Pressuring them would tend to polarise, or add to the polarisation of, central and local government, without a useful result to show for it — an outcome surely not in the interests of the work that is at issue here.

It is not only central government that is called on for restraint. Social workers have to be more modest in their claims of effectiveness. There is very little assurance of a desirable outcome in treating child abusers; and abused children, though they can be protected and may be helped, rarely emerge unscathed. Nothing in this says that professional skills should not be applied, but treatment techniques are not likely appreciably to reduce child abuse. It takes forbearance to decline to be thought better than one is; nevertheless, in the end it would be constructive.

The media also need to understand that PSS staff are dealing with a very imperfect science in making judgements whether abuse is likely to occur or whether fostering would be an improvement for a child. Short of taking thousands of children into care (which would also carry a cost for the children), there is no way to avoid taking risks based on workers' best judgement. When a decision turns out badly, one wants to know that the social worker was attentive and thoughtful, but it would be unreasonable to expect every decision to turn out well. Magistrates have now been given considerably more responsibility for these decisions; they will share the risk of opprobrium that social workers have faced and they are entitled to the same forbearance.

PSS staff have much to think about — the relationship between authority and partnership in child care, the relationship between client need and local authority resources with respect to all clients, the meaning of social class in emerging professional relationships, the forging of collaboration among professions which the new structures might tend to drive apart (in pitting one budget-holder against another, for example). What professional social work is at its core is tested in a variety of ways by the new law and guidance, and for the process of thinking it through staff must be given time and venue. Professional associations and educational and training institutions ought to be working out with PSS staff what social work stands for. This is a time that demands the exercise of professional and academic leadership — or what are they for?

Diversion

One message that this paper seeks to convey is that too many people with too great needs are being directed to the PSS. It is as if all the trees in a watershed were being chopped down and the people along the stream below were asked to build dikes higher, and still higher. Strategies have to be found upstream to reduce or prevent the downstream flood.

Too many people with too great needs are being directed to the PSS

Recommendations

National Health Service

One strategy would be to expect the NHS to slow the pace of hospital discharge. Quicker discharges from acute care are the rule now, and long-term beds are being emptied as fast as possible. In making these decisions, in many and perhaps in most cases, physicians deal with relativities and judgements about risk and it is clear that, in general, they have moved to taking somewhat higher risks. It does not simplify these decisions that physicians must deal with social as well as medical judgements: Will this patient be able to care for himself? Is care or support available at home?

There is so far little evidence of the net medical effect of this shift in standards about acceptable risk, but there *is* evidence that many discharged patients experience pain and considerable difficulty in managing (2). It would be good for the patients and ease the work of the PSS if the NHS were prepared to keep patients somewhat longer — when social and medical judgements justify this, of course. The British Medical Association has offered a similar recommendation (3). Health authorities and local authorities might, indeed, agree a 'joint user' approach, with shared costs for a specified number of long-stay beds. Such agreements might avoid the "potential minefield" in relationships between health and local authorities that community care poses (4).

Graded age and disability pensions

In modern times, a critical problem of ageing and disability lies in feelings about losing command over one's self and surroundings. The issue has to do with changes in bodily functioning, with the loss of power once exercised through position or work, and with the loss of power in relation to family and friends. Some of these changes are inevitable but modern practices enforce an abrupt transition, once uncommon, from power to powerlessness.

If it is plausible that government policy ought to support rather than undermine the elderly or disabled person's sense of control over herself or her own resources, one is led to question the pot-pourri of programmes with which the government provides assistance for carers. The elderly or disabled person may receive a non-means-tested allowance, with the amount related to how much care is needed. Carers for such people may receive a relatively modest invalid care allowance as well. Then, a comparatively small number who need a great deal of care may receive substantial grants from the Independent Living Fund — but this programme appears about to be wound up. And finally, there is the new Disability Living Allowance, for people who need help but not so much as would qualify them for the Attendance Allowance.

One effect of these programmes is that others — PSS staff, family members, carers — determine the arrangements of elderly and disabled people. This is precisely what people who already feel undermined do not need. Besides, this case-by-case method of determination makes for expensive administration and leads to problems of take-up (5).

However, money placed in the hands of elderly and disabled people can create quite a different situation, in which they decide their own arrangements. Generally speaking, a plausible argument can be made for reworking pension levels to pay less at sixty or sixty-five, more at seventy-five, and even more at the age

The pace of hospital discharge might be slowed

The personal social services

Funds will need to match expectations

of eighty-five. With advancing age, attendance is more likely to be needed, other needs tend to increase and resources tend to be depleted. Benefits levels may be reasonably, if roughly, adjusted. If this were done, attendance and carers' allowances for the elderly would simply fold into the benefit formula.

The changeover would not be made by actually reducing anyone's benefit, of course. The changeover could be accomplished over time by differentially redirecting cost of living increases, with government money that had been spent on attendance also used for the upgraded benefits. The 'young old' should not be outraged at the change, as they may hope to benefit when they in their turn become older.

A hypothetical example of this sort of shift, worked out for the United States in 1979, produced benefit levels of $276 a month for those from 65 to 74 years old, $332 a month for those up to 84 years of age, and $359 a month for those over 85 — *without added cost* (6). (Average benefit levels are now approximately twice as high as in 1979, so the increments would also have doubled.)

With respect to a constant attendance allowance for younger people who are disabled, it is harder to provide simple, rough justice. Probably, the determination of entitlement ought to be based on the medical record that establishes entitlement to invalidity benefit, with severity of disability determining the level of increased payment.

A number of issues arise which, for the purposes of this paper, I do not address (7). The point here is that one could use social security greatly to simplify current provision and to provide choice and control to claimants. In the process, people would make their own arrangements about community care, *without having to resort to PSS*. Some would not be able to manage even so; as now, they would be able to seek help from PSS.

Diversion, in conclusion

These two proposals — not so much haste in hospital discharges and graded age and disability pensions — by no means exhaust the possibilities of dealing with the problems of people through other social institutions before they must turn to PSS for personal and, in a sense, handicraft attention. Relatively speaking, these are not expensive solutions, at least when one takes into account what they would cost if the same people were to come to PSS. Government working parties, involving the Ministries of Health and Social Security and of the Environment and voluntary organisations might give thought to the development of a repertoire of similar ideas.

Resources

PSS have been short of funds for fifteen years, or so, and are now asked to assume large new responsibilities (see Section 4). Funds will have to be provided in magnitudes proportionate to what is being asked. It is not possible, in the framework of this paper, to do a detailed analysis of funding. However, it seems evident that additional funds in a range from £500 million to £1,000 million need to be provided, the increment to be arrived at over a period of two or three years. I arrive at this broad conclusion in the following manner.

The Local Authority Associations (LAA) have done their own analysis of what additional resources are needed for England and, depending on one set of assumptions and

Recommendations

another, arrive at figures ranging from £430 to £479 million (**8**).

These figures are an understatement in several important respects. The calculation is based on needs for 1991-1992, and so does not include the greatly increased costs that will result from full implementation of care management. It counts on transfer of social security money now being spent for residential care, but does not calculate the effect of the shortfall between transfers and the actual charges for residential care which will be current. The £5 million sum it allocates for dealing with the so-called 'Staffordshire effect' (the effect of publicity about scandalous treatment of children in residential care) is derisory. A review of *Children in the Public Care* (**9**) makes it clear that much more will have to be spent.

The £400-plus million figure does not include separately stated capital expenditures — an item that comes to several hundred million pounds, by one calculation and another. Particularly to be noted is the expectation that in order to implement community care in the ways that guidance proposes, a large sum would need to be spent on information technology. It is perhaps helpful to recall that reorganisation of the NHS was accompanied by a large investment in information systems. And finally, LAA's estimate for England has to be expanded to the United Kingdom.

Plainly, the LAA analysis represents a position in a negotiation that was to take place with central government; one recognises this. On the other hand, it is not possible to review the document without grasping that a deficit accumulated over fifteen years is being dealt with; and the magnitude of the needs that were *not* incorporated. Even if one reduces LAA's estimate by 25 per cent, it would still be evident that a painstaking and realistic figure, taking all needs into account, would have to exceed £500 million and might well reach £1,000 million.

Support provided by central government would presumably be divided among local authorities in accordance with measures of local need, and there has of course been great dissatisfaction with the formulation of the standard spending assessment. The growth of central government support to (currently) 86 per cent of local budgets also raises questions about the purposes of and relative autonomy accorded to local authorities.

A considerable case can be made that, in the longer run — that is, two, three, or four years — the financial relationship between central government and local authorities should be revised. The Joseph Rowntree Foundation's Local and Central Government Research Committee has proposed institution of a local government income tax which, together with the Council tax, would provide half of local government revenue (**10**). Others may offer proposals as well, but the question of financing needs basic reconsideration.

In any event, very substantial additional support needs to be provided to the PSS — urgently. In the event that this is not to be then, certainly, charge-capping needs to be re-examined. If financial support is adequate, charge-capping is arguably sound policy — assuring fair and uniform provision across the country. When support is not adequate, charge-capping means levelling *down* and is poor policy. Furthermore, if substantial additional support is not provided, then the government needs to reconsider the objectives it has set out

The PSS need very substantial support — urgently

The personal social services

for PSS, balancing wishes against resources, and arrive at a mission that is reasonably realisable. "Wishing will make it so" is a song that may summon up nostalgia but was never sound policy and, in this context, is entirely mischievous.

This point is not merely rhetorical; it is important. Let me put it more baldly: Jean Packman and Bill Jordan have pointed to the "astonishing echoes" in the Children Act of the Ingleby Report of thirty years ago (11). Setting out to support families, it brought a "deluge" of referrals but provided minimal resources, producing a variety of adverse effects on service delivery.

Similarly, the current drive for community care is not a departure from earlier policies but rather a continuation of a thirty-year record of responding to failure to achieve stated goals by setting ever more grandiose goals without making those goals realisable. If the work of PSS is to be made feasible, the resources must be provided to do the work.

If this cannot be done, the goals must be adjusted to available resources.

Last words

The personal social services are at a critical stage. They were established with high hopes, flourished briefly, and then were subjected to a variety of internal and external strains. In the view of the public, certainly, they have failed to deliver with respect to important national objectives — protecting children and fostering community care, for two examples. They are now seriously malfunctioning.

It is the conclusion here that the PSS must now be given room and resources for collecting themselves to meet the challenges that have been set for them. Restraint, diversion and resources are the recommendations offered. Failing these, PSS will probably decline into a state of disorganisation from which recovery will be all but impossible. These are harsh words — some people think they should not be voiced; but it appears that they state the problem exactly.

The PSS may become so disorganised that recovery is impossible

> **NOTE**
> It is perhaps illuminating that, among readers of a draft of this report, some who are furthest from the front lines have found it depressing and fear that it may provide an excuse for giving up. On the other hand, line workers have seemed to find relief and encouragement in the report. They had felt isolated and alone in their perception of the difficulties; nor are they so far disposed to give up. I believe, however, that time is short.

Notes

Introduction

1 Alvin L Schorr, *Slums and Social Insecurity*, Thomas Nelson and Sons, 1964.

Chapter 1: Background

1 Joan Cooper, *The Creation of the British Personal Social Services, 1962-74*, Heinemann Education Books, 1983.

2 Adrian Webb and Gerald Wistow, *Planning, Need and Scarcity, Essays on the Personal Social Services,* Allen and Unwin, 1986; Peter Townsend, *The Fifth Social Service*, Fabian Society, 1971.

3 Frederic Seebohm, 'The Seebohm Reorganisation: What went wrong', in Frederic Seebohm, *Seebohm Twenty Years On*, Policy Studies Institute, 1989.

4 Webb and Wistow, 1986, *op. cit.*

5 Robert Pinker, 'Social Work and Social Policy in the Twentieth Century: Retrospect and prospect', in Martin Bulmer, Jane Lewis and David Piachaud, *The Goals of Social Policy*, Unwin Hyman, 1989.

6 Peter M Barclay, chairman of working party set up at request of Secretary of State for Social Services, *Social Workers, Their Role and Tasks,* National Institute for Social Work, Bedford Square Press, 1982; Sir Roy Griffiths, *Community Care: Agenda for action*, A report to the Secretary of State for Social Services, HMSO, 1988.

7 Tessa Jowell, 'Challenges and Opportunities', *Conference Speeches Delivered by Virginia Bottomley and Tessa Jowell*, distributed with *Caring for People*, issue number 4, 1991.

8 Peter Westland, 'Success or Failure — the UK's approach to social welfare', Conference in Madrid, 22-24 January, 1990. Typescript.

9 Robert Pinker, *Social Work in an Enterprise Society*, Routledge, 1990, p. 125.

10 For an early critique of the idea of the 'new poor' see Bill Jordan, *Paupers*, Routledge and Kegan Paul, 1973.

Chapter 2: Clients and their resources

1 Saul Becker, *Windows of Opportunity*, Child Poverty Action Group, 1991.

2 Robert Walker and Geoffrey Hardman, 'The Financial Resources of the Elderly or Paying Your Own Way in Old Age', in Sally Baldwin, Gillian Parker, Robert Walker, eds, *Social Security and Community Care*, Avebury, 1988.

3 Janet Ford, *Consuming Credit*, Child Poverty Action Group, 1991.

4 British Council of Organisations of Disabled People, 'Disabled People and Institutional Discrimination', *Social Policy Research Findings* No 21, Joseph Rowntree Foundation 1991; Robert Walker and Gillian Parker, *Money Matters — Income, wealth and financial welfare*, Sage Publications, 1988.

5 Department of Health, *Patterns and Outcomes in Child Placement*, HMSO, 1991.

6 Saul Becker and Stewart MacPherson, *Poor Clients*, Department of Social Administration and Social Work, University of Nottingham, May 1986.

7 Christine Oldman, 'Personal Sources of Funding Care', *Social Policy Research Findings* No 20, Joseph Rowntree Foundation 1991.

8 There is a view among some experts and practitioners that only a small proportion of the poor use PSS and *they* tend to use the services over and over. There is some difference about this, and I was not able to establish it definitively. It would, in fact, be important to know, having implications for the kind and degree of special training staff should have, and posing a policy issue about the degree to which the departments wish to be engaged in preventive service.

9 Nicholas Barr and Fiona Coulter, 'Social Security: Solution or problem', in *The State of Welfare: The welfare state in Britain since 1974*, Oxford University Press, 1990.

10 Janet Finch, 'Social Policy, Social Engineering and the Family in the 1990s', in Bulmer, 1989, *op. cit.*

11 Dermot Clifford, *The Social Costs and Rewards of Caring*, Avebury 1990.

12 Martin Bulmer, *Neighbours: The work of Philip Abrams*, Cambridge University Press, 1986; see also Gillian Parker, 'They've Got Their Own Lives to Lead: Carers and dependent people talking about family and neighbourhood help', in J Hutton, S Hutton, T Pinch and A Shiell, eds, *Dependency and Enterprise,* Routledge, 1991; Oldman, 1991, *op. cit.*; Clifford, 1990, *op. cit.*; Caroline Glendinning, *A Single Door*, Allen and Unwin, 1986; Walker, 1988, *op. cit.*; Finch, 1989, *op cit.*

13 Bulmer, 1986, p.230, *op cit.*

14 For example, see Isobel Allen, Malcolm Wicks, Janet Finch, Diana Leat, *Informal Care Tomorrow*, Policy Studies Institute, 1986, p.4.

15 Hazel Green, *Informal Carers*, OPCS, General Household Survey 1985, Series GH5, No 15, Supplement A, HMSO, 1988.

16 Bulmer, 1986, *op. cit.*; Finch, 1989, *op. cit.*

17 Diana Leat, 'Using Social Security Payments to Encourage Non-kin Caring', in Baldwin, 1988, *op. cit.*

18 Pinker, 1990, *op. cit.*

19 Alvin L Schorr, '... Thy Father and Thy Mother ...', A

The personal social services

Second Look at Filial Responsibility and Family Policy, US Social Security Administration, July 1980, p.3, GPO 1980.

20 Parker, 1991, *op. cit.*

21 Marie Jahoda, *Employment and Unemployment*, Cambridge University Press, 1982, p.3; see also Joint Working Party of Directors of Social Services and the Welsh Office, 'The Implications of Rising Unemployment for Personal Social Services in Wales', March 1981, mimeograph; Finch, 1989, *op. cit.*, p.94; Adrian Sinfield, 'The Impact of Unemployment under Different Policy Responses', paper presented at the First European Dialogue on Social Policies, Helsinki, 15-19 March 1990.

22 Jane Gibbons, speech delivered at the National Institute for Social Work conference on 'Family Support and the Children Act', November 1991; Jonathan Bradshaw and Jane Millar, *Lone Parents Families in the UK*, Department of Social Security Research Report No 6, HMSO 1991; Glendinning, 1986, *op. cit.*; Alan Murie, 'Housing, Homelessness and Social Work' in Saul Becker and Stewart MacPherson, eds, *Public Issues, Private Pain*, Care Matters Ltd, London 1988; Gary Craig, 'Unmet Need and the Social Fund', paper presented at jointly organised conference of the National Children's Bureau and Family Service Units, 20 November 1991; Baldwin, 1988, *op. cit.*; Jonathan Bradshaw, 'The Social Impact of Childhood Disablement', *Kinderchirurgie*, v 43, Supplement II, Stuttgart, 1988; Finch, 1989 *op. cit.*; Roy Parker, a summary of the proceeding presented at a conference on 'Family Support and the Children Act' at the National Institute for Social Work, 11 November, 1991; Roger Smith, paper presented at jointly organised conference of the National Children's Bureau and Family Service Units, 20 November 1991.

23 Roy Parker, 1991, *op. cit.*; Dione Hills, *Carer Support in the Community*, Department of Health, Social Services Inspectorate, 1991.

24 Hills, 1991, *op. cit.*; Isobel Allen, Debra Hogg, Sheila Peace, *Elderly People — Choice, Participation and Satisfaction*, Policy Studies Institute, 1992, p. 301.

25 Gibbons, 1991, *op. cit.*; Pinker, 1990, *op. cit.*; Stewart MacPherson, 'Getting By and Getting Through', in Becker, 1988, *op. cit.*; Craig, 1991, *op. cit.*

26 Janet Finch, 'Social Policy, Social Engineering and the Family in the 1990s', in Bulmer, 1989, *op. cit.*; Finch, *Family Obligations ...*, 1989, *op. cit.*; Parker, 1991, *op. cit..* See also Peter Townsend, *The Family Life of Old People*, Routledge and Kegan Paul, 1957; Schorr, 1980, *op. cit.*

27 Parker, 'Tending and Social Policy', in *A New Look at the Personal Social Services*, E Matilda Goldberg and Stephen Hatch, eds, Policy Studies Institute, 1981, p.22.

28 Finch 1989, *Family Obligations ...*, *op. cit.* p.243.

29 Alvin L Schorr, *Filial Responsibility in the Modern American Family*, US Social Security Administration, Division of Program Research, GPO, 1961.

30 Allen, 1986, *op. cit.*; Caroline Glendinning, 'Impoverishing Women', in Alan Walker and Carol Walker, eds, *The Growing Divide; A social audit, 1979-1987*, Child Poverty Action Group, 1987.

Chapter 3: The economic environment

1 David Thomson, 'Workhouse to Nursing Home: Residential care of elderly people in England since 1840', *Ageing and Society*, v 3, part 1, pp 43-69, March 1983.

2 Robert M Moroney, *The Family and State: Considerations for Social Policy*, Longman, London, 1976.

3 Thomson, 1983, *op. cit.*, p. 67.

4 *Ibid.*

5 Ian Sinclair, *Homes for the Elderly*, Independent Review of Residential Care, processed, no publisher, undated.

6 BMA, *Priorities for Community Care*, British Medical Association, 1992.

7 Schorr, 1980, *op. cit.*

8 Respectively House of Commons, Social Security Committee, First Report, *Low Income Statistics: households Below Average Income, Tables 1988*, 1991, Table H1; Table F1; Becker, 1991, *op. cit.* Table 2; House of Commons, 1991, *op. cit.*, p. 6; Peter Townsend, 1991, *The Poor are Poorer: A statistical report on changes in the living standards of rich and poor in the United Kingdom 1979-1989*, Department of Social Policy and Social Planning, University of Bristol, March 1991, Table 2.

9 House of Commons, 1991, p. vii.

10 Martha R Burt, 'Roots and Remedies of Homelessness', *Policy and Research Report*, v 21, no 2, Summer 1991, The Urban Institute, Washington DC, based on Martha R Burt, *Over the Edge: The growth of Homelessness in the 1980s*, Urban Institute Press and Russell Sage Foundation, Washington DC and New York City, 1991.

11 R G Wilkinson, 'Income Distribution and Life Expectancy', *British Medical Journal*, v 304, 18 January 1992.

12 Becker, 1991, *op. cit.* Table 2.

13 Will Hutton, 'Conservatives Avoid the Most Taxing Question', citing National Children's Home study, *The Guardian*, 7 October 1991.

14 House of Commons, 1991, *op. cit.*, Table G.

15 A B Atkinson, *Poverty and Social Security*, Harvester

Notes

Wheatsheaf, 1989, pp. 142-145.

16 David Kirk, Sarah Nelson, Adrian and Dorothy Sinfield, *Excluding Youth — Poverty among young people living away from home*, Bridges Project: Edinburgh Centre for Social Welfare Research, University of Edinburgh, March 1991; see also Jill Vincent, 'The Conservatives' Diary', Appendix in Becker, 1991, *op. cit.*

17 Atkinson, 1989, *op. cit.*

18 Jane Millar, 'Bearing the Cost' in Becker, 1991, *op. cit.* p.31.

19 John Hills, *How the Tax System Works and How to Change It*, Child Poverty Action Group, 1988, p. 13.

20 Barr, 1990, *op. cit.*

21 *Annual Abstract of Statistics*, Central Statistical Office, 1980, Table 15.1; *Annual Abstract of Statistics*, Central Statistical Office, 1991, Table 15.1.

22 Barr, 1990, *op. cit.*

23 *The Guardian*, 7 Jan 1992, p.2.

24 House of Commons, 1991, *op.cit.*, Table F1.

25 *Ibid.*

26 Age Concern England, 'Moving the Goalposts', *Briefings*, London, December 1989; Age Concern England, 'Income Support for Residential and Nursing Home Care', Submission to the Social Security Select Committee, April 19 1991, with Supplement May 16, 1991.

27 House of Commons, 1991, *op. cit.* Table A2

28 *What Price the Nation's Children?*, National Children's Bureau, 1992, p. 6.

29 *The Guardian*, 7 Jan 1992, p.2.

30 Hammersmith and Fulham, *Social Services Community Care Plan*, 1991-92

31 Child Poverty Action Group (CPAG), *Working Against Poverty*, Annual Report 1991.

32 Richard Berthoud, 'The Social Fund — Is it working?', *Policy Studies*, v 12, No 1, 1991; Smith, 1991, *op. cit.*

33 *Inquiry into British Housing: Second Report, June 1991*, chaired by HRH the Duke of Edinburgh, Joseph Rowntree Foundation, 1991, p.13.

34 Hammersmith and Fulham, 1991-92.

35 *Inquiry*, 1991, *op. cit.*, p. 26.

36 *Inquiry*, 1991, *op. cit.*, Figure 8; Diane Boliver, 'Missing Millions of Income Support Could Solve Problem of Defaulters, Say Lenders', *The Guardian*, 17 December 1991; Steven Webb and Steve Wilcox, 'Mortgage benefit for low-income home-owners', *Housing Research Findings* No, 51, Joseph Rowntree Foundation, 1991.

37 *Inquiry*, 1991, *op. cit.*, Figure 7; Will Hutton, 'Housing Is Where Recovery Is', *The Guardian* 23 September 1991.

38 Richard Best, 'Community Care and Housing Associations', in Baldwin, 1988, *op. cit.*, p. 37.

39 John Greve, 'Increases in Homelessness', *Housing Research Findings* No 45, Joseph Rowntree Foundation, 1991, p. 3.

40 Duncan Maclennan *Search*, No 10, August, Joseph Rowntree Foundation, 1991.

41 Burt, 1991, *op. cit.*

42 *Inquiry*, 1991, *op. cit.*, Figures 1 and 2.

43 *Ibid*, Figure 2.

44 *Ibid.*

45 Angela Evans, 'Temporary Housing for Homeless People', *Housing Research Findings* No 50, Joseph Rowntree Foundation, 1991.

46 Kirk, 1991, *op cit.*

47 *Ibid.*

48 Atkinson, 1989, *op. cit.*, p. 88.

49 Eithne McLaughlin, 'Work and Welfare Benefits: Social Security, Employment and Unemployment in the 1990s', *Journal of Social Policy*, v 20, part 4, October 1991, p. 487; Carey Oppenheim, *Poverty the Facts*, Child Poverty Action Group, 1990.

50 McLaughlin, 1991, *op. cit.*

51 Hutton, Oct. 91, *op. cit.*

52 Keith Harper, ' "Low Pay" Plight of 10 Million Workers', *The Guardian*, 14 January 1992.

53 *Ibid.*

54 McLaughlin, 1991, *op. cit.*

55 See Kirk, 1991, *op. cit.* Oppenheim, 1990, *op. cit.*

Chapter 4: Funding

1 Maria Evandrou, Jane Falkingham and Howard Glennerster, 'The Personal Social Services: Everyone's Poor Relation but Nobody's Baby', in Hills *op. cit.*; Tessa Harding, *Great Expectations and Spending on Social Services*, NISW Policy Forum Paper No 1, January, National Institute for Social Work, 1992.

2 Linda Challis, *Organising Public Social Services*, Longman, 1990.

3 Maria Evandrou, *Challenging the Invisibility of Carers: Mapping informal care nationally*, STICERD, WSP/49, September, London School of Economics, 1990; Webb, 1986, *op. cit.*

4 Department of Health, unpublished tables, 1992.

5 Harding, 1992, *op. cit.*, Chapter 3.

The personal social services

6 Harding, 1992, *op. cit.*; National Audit Office, *Community Care Developments,* HMSO 1987.

7 *Poverty*, Winter, 1991, p.3.

8 Howard Glennerster, 'The Planning Process', *Community Care*, July 11, 1991

9 Challis, 1990, *op. cit.*

10 Sir William Utting, *Children in the Public Care: A review of residential child care,* HMSO, 1991.

11 Herbert Laming, quoted in *The Guardian*, 11 November 1991.

12 Adrian Barritt, *Innovations in Community Care,* Family Policy Studies Centre, occasional paper, September, 1990, pp. 42-43.

13 Jane Tunstill, 'The Children Act and the Voluntary Childcare Sector', *Children and Society*, v 5, No 1, 1991, p.81.

14 House of Commons, 28 February 1990.

15 David Brindle, 'Councils Face Care-funding Gap of £130m', *The Guardian*, 31 March 1991.

16 Bradshaw, 1988, *op. cit.*, p. 179.

17 June Neill and Jenny Williams, *Elderly People Leaving Hospital: A study of discharge to community care*, National Institute for Social Work, September, 1991. BMA, 1992, *op. cit.*, para 258.

18 *The Lancet*, 1 February 1992, p. 294; BMA, 1992, *op. cit.*, paras. 2.44, 3.3, 3.4.

19 *The Lancet*, January 11, 1992, p. 96

20 House of Commons, Social Services Committee, *Community Care: Funding for local authorities*, 7 March, HMSO, 1990; House of Commons, Social Services Committee, *Community Care: Minutes of evidence*, 17 July, HMSO, 1990, p. 2, testimony of Virginia Bottomley.

21 David J Hunter, 'An Overview of Community Care in Britain: Mixed experiences and mixed economics', in M Ulas, S Black and P Hambleton, eds, *Community Care: A mixed economy*, Social Services Research Group, 1990, p.5.

22 Oldman, 1991, *op. cit.* p.5

Chapter 5: 'Cognitive dissonance'

1 Leon Festinger, 'The Theory of Cognitive Dissonance', in Wilbur Schramm, *The Science of Human Communication*, Basic Books, 1963, p. 17.

2 *Caring For People, Implementation Documents*, 'Draft Guidance: Assessment and case management', CCI, 8, Department of Health (DoH), undated, 3.3.2

3 Challis, 1990, *op. cit.*, p. 84.

4 House of Commons, Social Services Committee, *Community Care: Planning and co-operation,* May 1990, p. 305

5 Mike Oliver, 'Civil Rights, Disability and Citizenship: A case of disabling welfare', Paper presented to Social Services Policy Forum, undated typescript, Thames Polytechnic, 1992; Mike Oliver and Colin Barnes, 'Discrimination, Disability and Welfare: From needs to rights', undated typescript, Thames Polytechnic; Michael Oliver, *The Politics of Disablement*, Macmillan, 1990.

6 DoH, *Caring For People, Implementation Documents*, undated, para. 25.

7 DoH, *The Government's Plans for the Future of Community Care,* Presented to Parliament by the Secretary of State for Health, November, HMSO, 1990.

8 Association of County Councils (ACC), *Caring for People: Meeting the challenge*, 1990, p. 8.

9 ACC, 'Community Care '91: The county experience', *Briefing*, Typescript, 1991.

10 Simon Biggs, 'Case Management in Community Care, Advantages and Disadvantages', in Thompson and Mathias, eds, *Helping People Who Experience Mental Handicap: Keys to Competence*, Harcourt, Brace Jovanovich, 1991.

11 Oldman, 1991, *op. cit.*

12 Allen, 1992, *op. cit.*, p. 311.

13 Raymond Jack, 'Case Management and Social Services: Welfare or trade fair?', *Generations Review*, v 2, No 1, March, 1992.

14 BMA, 1992, *op. cit.*, p. 230.

15 Jean Packman and Bill Jordan, 'The Children Act: Looking forward, looking back', *British Journal of Social Work*, August, v 21, 1991, p. 319.

16 Report of the Inquiry into the circumstances surrounding the death of Jasmine Beckford, *A Child in Trust*, London Borough of Brent, 1985, p 12; see also Pinker, 1990, *op. cit.*, p.90 ff.

17 Lorraine Fox Harding, *Perspectives in Child Care Policy*, Longman, 1991, p.217.

18 Packman, 1991, *op. cit.*,p.323

19 Walker, 1991, *op. cit.*

20 Margaret Adcock *et al.*, *Significant Harm*, Significant Publications, 1991.

21 For examples, see a professional discussion of why, over the years, children's parents have lacked power vis-à-vis social service departments (DoH, 1991, *op. cit.*, pp.44-46); and the report of a study of case conferences (June

Notes

Thoburn, Ann Lewis and David Shemmings, *Family Involvement in Child Protection Conference*, Discussion paper 1, Social Work Development Unit, University of East Anglia, 1991).

22 Thoburn, 1991, *op. cit.*, p. 5.

23 Home Office, Department of Health, Department of Education and Science, Welsh Office, *Working Together under the Children Act 1989*, HMSO, 1991, para. 5.17.

24 Jo Tunnard and Mary Ryan, 'What Does the Children Act Mean for Family Members?', *Children and Society*, v 5, No 1, Spring, 1991, p. 67.

25 DoH, 1991, *op. cit.* p.44ff; Joel F Handler, *The Coercive Social Worker*, Rand McNally College Publishing Company, 1973.

26 Lorraine Fox Harding, *Perspectives in Child Care Policy*, Longman, 1991, p.229.*op. cit.*

27 DoH, 1991, *op. cit.* p. 45.

28 Tunnard, 1991, *op. cit.*

29 *Caring for People, Community Care in the Next Decade and Beyond*, Presented to Parliament by the Secretaries of State for Health, Social Security, Wales and Scotland, November, HMSO, Cm. 849, 1989, 1.3.

30 House of Commons, Health Committee, Second Report, *Public Expenditure of Public Social Services: Child Protection Services*, v 1, 3 July 1991, pp. iv to viii.

31 Tunstill, 1991, *op. cit.*, p. 82.

32 House of Commons, May 1990, *op. cit.*, p. 307.

33 Allen, 1992, *op. cit.* pp. 301 ff.

34 *Caring for People*, 1989, 3.2.12.

35 'Stranded in a Careless Community', *The Independent*, 16 Feb 1992.

36 *Caring for People*, 1989, 3.2.12.

37 Finch, 'Social Policy ...', 1989, *op. cit.*

Chapter 6: The Children Act and child abuse

1 *A Child in Trust*, Brent, *op. cit.*, p. 10.

2 Susan J Creighton and Philip Noyes, *Child Abuse Trends in England and Wales, 1983-87*, National Society for Prevention of Cruelty to Children, 1989, p. 45.

3 Ian White, 'Taking a Look at the Year Ahead', *Community Care*, January, 1992, p. 11.

4 Creighton, 1989, *op. cit.*; *Report of Inquiry into Child Abuse in Cleveland, 1987*, Presented to Parliament by the Secretary of State for Social Services, July, 1988; Jean La Fontaine, *Child Sexual Abuse*, Polity Press, 1990.

5 Cleveland, 1988, *op. cit.* p. 5.

6 Theresa M McBride, 'Social Mobility for the Lower Classes: Domestic servants in France', *The Journal of Social History*, Fall, 1974; Anne Martin-Fugier, *La Place des Bonnes: La Domesticité feminine à Paris en 1900*, B Grosset, 1979.

7 Cleveland, 1988, *op. cit.* p. 5.

8 'Social Worker "Ashamed of His Conduct in Children's Home" ', *The Guardian*, 15 November 1991.

9 Barbara Nelson, *Making an Issue of Child Abuse*, University of Chicago Press, 1984.

10 DoH, *Child Abuse: A Study of Inquiry Reports, 1980-1989*, HMSO, 1991, p. 110.

11 La Fontaine, 1990, *op. cit.*, p. 209.

12 Pinker, 1990, *op. cit.*, Chap 6.

13 La Fontaine, 1990, *op. cit.*

14 DoH, *Personal Social Services, LA Statistics, Children in Care of Local Authorities, Year Ending 31 March 1989, England*, HMSO, 1991; *Personal Social Services, LA Statistics, Children in Care of Local Authorities, Year Ending 31 March 1990, England*, 1991.

15 DoH, *Patterns and Outcomes ...*, 1991, *op. cit.*, p. 7; also 'Children at Risk in Homes', British Medical Journal, 304, No 6824, 15 February, 1992, p. 403; Judith Harwin, 'Child Protection and the Role of the Social Worker Under the Children Act 1989', unpublished typescript, London School of Economics, 1992, pp. 2-3.

16 Cleveland, 1988, *op. cit.*, p. 245

Chapter 7: Cost-effectiveness, assessment and care management

1 House of Commons, 17 July 1990, *op. cit.*, testimony of Virginia Bottomley, p. 2.

2 Hazel Qureshi, personal communication, April 1992.

3 National Audit Office, *Developing Community Care for Adults without Mental Handicap*, Occasional Papers No 9, October, HMSO 1989; Sinclair, undated, *op. cit.*, p. 5; Ian Sinclair, *Residential Care: The research reviewed*, National Institute for Social Work, HMSO, 1988, p. 24; Roy Parker in Sinclair, 1988, *op. cit.*, pp. 8 to 15.

4 Schorr, 1980, *op. cit.*, p. 33.

5 The Audit Commission for Local Authorities in England and Wales, *Managing Social Services for the Elderly More Effectively*, HMSO, 1985.

6 Sinclair, undated, *op. cit.*, p.21.

7 House of Commons, May 1990, *op. cit.*, p. 307; see also Social Services Inspectorate, Department of Health, *Inspection of Community Social Services for Elderly People with Mental Disorder*, undated, (1988?).

8 Newcastle City Council, Social Services Committee,

The personal social services

Minutes, 24 April, 1992, duplicated, pp. 37ff; Hazel Qureshi, 'Social Care Services for Disabled People', in Gillian Daley, ed, *Disability and Social Policy*, PSI Publishing, 1991.

9 National Audit Office, October 1989, *op. cit.*;

10 Bleddyn Davies *et al.*, *Resources, Needs and Outcomes in Community Services: An overview*, PSSRU, University of Kent at Canterbury, June, 1989; Peter Gorbach, 'Clarifying the Framework', National Institute for Social Work, January, typescript, 1991; Allen, 1992, *op. cit.*

11 Bleddyn Davies, *Resources, Needs and Outcomes in Community-based Care ...: The messages distilled; a commentary*, University of Kent at Canterbury, January, 1991.

12 Bulmer, 1986, *op. cit.*, p. 239.

13 T Franklin Williams, letter, *The Lancet*, 19 August 1978; J C Brocklehurst, M H C McCarty, J T Leeming and J M Robinson, 'Medical Screening of Old People Accepted for Residential Care', *The Lancet*, 15 July, 1978.

14 David Challis and Bleddyn Davies, 'Long-term Care for the Elderly: The community care scheme', *British Journal of Social Work*, 15, 1985; David Challis and Bleddyn Davies, *Case Management in Community Care* Gower, 1986; David Challis, R Barton, L Johnson, M Stone, K Traske and B Wall, *Supporting Frail Elderly People at Home*, PSS Research Unit, University of Kent at Canterbury, 1989; Paul Cambridge, *From Micro-Budgeting to Agency Pluralism: Some lessons from the care in the community initiative*, PSS Research Unit, University of Kent at Canterbury, typescript, 1988; Davies, 1986, *op. cit.*.

15 Ann Richardson and Ray Higgins, *Care Management in Practice: Reflections on the Wakefield Case Management Project*, working paper 1, Nuffield Institute for Health Services Studies, University of Leeds, April 1990, processed; Gillian Parker, 'Whose Care, Whose Costs? Whose Benefit? A critical review of research in case management and informal care', *Ageing and Society*, v 10, 1990, pp 459-467; see also Biggs, 1991, *op. cit.*; Jack, 1992, *op. cit.*; Qureshi, 1991, *op. cit.*

16 Davies, 1989, *op. cit.* p.10.

17 Davies, 1991, *op. cit.*

18 Peter Willmott, *Community Initiatives, Patterns and Prospects*, Policy Studies Institute, 1989, p.59.

19 *Caring for People*, 1989, para 3.2.12.

20 Gorbach, 1991, *op. cit.*, p. 1.

21 Nirmala Rao, *From Providing to Enabling: Local authorities and community care planning*, Joseph Rowntree Foundation, 1991, p. 35.

22 Jack Rothman, 'A Model of Care Management: Toward empirically-based practice', *Social Work*, (Silver Spring, Maryland), November, v 36, no 6, pp 520-528, 1991.

23 Esther Wattenberg, 'Minor Mothers and Welfare Reform,' *Public Welfare* (Washington DC), v 49, No 4, Fall, 1991, pp 12-21.

24 Jerry Spann, *The Community Options Program (COP): A public choice for personal choice in long-term support*, The Robert M La Follette Institute of Public Affairs, University of Wisconsin, Spring, 1987.

25 *Ibid.*

26 James J Callahan, Jr, 'Case Management for the Elderly: A panacea?', *Journal of Aging and Social Policy,* 1, 1/2, 1989, p. 181; p. 189.

27 British Association of Social Workers, *Community Care: Whose choice?*, A policy statement from the British Association of Social Workers, Birmingham.

28 Challis, 1990, *op. cit.*

29 Callahan, 1989, *op. cit.*

30 Michael O'Higgins, 'Strategy Options for Devolved Financial Management in Community Care,' Presentation to the Welfare State Program Series, STICERD, London School of Economics, 12 February 1992.

31 Rao, 1991, *op. cit.*, p. 6.

32 Age Concern England, 1989, *op. cit.*, p. 1.

33 Circular letter form Andrew Foster, National Health Service, and Herbert Laming, Social Services Inspectorate, 11 March 1992.

34 DoH, *Health and Personal Social Services Statistics for England*, HMSO, 1991, Table 3.1.

Chapter 8: Brinksmanship in administration

1 J Goldstein, Anna Freud and Albert Solnit, *Beyond the Best Interests of the Child*, Free Press, 1973.

2 Alvin L Schorr, ed., *Cleveland Development: A dissenting view*, David Press, 1991, Chap. 6; see also Schorr, *Common Decency: Domestic policies after Reagan*, 1986, pp. 96 - 101.

3 Tunstill, 1991, *op. cit.*

4 Richard M Titmuss, *Commitment to Welfare*, George Allen and Unwin, 1968; Department of Health and Social Security, *Child Abuse: A study of inquiry reports, 1973-1981*, HMSO, 1982.

5 Linda Challis, 1990, *op. cit*, pp. vii, 14-15.

6 Ian White, 'Taking a Look at the Year Ahead,' *Community Care*, January 1992, p. 11.

7 Jowell, 1991, *op. cit.* p. 5.

8 Gibbons, 1991, *op. cit.*

Notes

9 National Audit Office, *People Management: Retaining and recruiting professionals,* Management Papers No 4, June, HMSO, 1989.

10 Ian White, 'Summary Comments', at National Institute for Social Work Conference on Family Support and the Children Act, London, 11 November, 1991.

11 National Audit Office, June, 1989, *op. cit.,* p. 2

12 Susan Balloch and Brian Jones, 'Social Services Responses to Poverty in Becker, 1988, *op. cit.*; Julie Ridley and Michael McCarthy, *Unemployment and the Personal Social Services*, British Association of Social Workers, 1986.

13 National Audit Office, June 1989, *op. cit.,* p. 2; Maria Evandrou, Jane Falkingham and Howard Glennerster, 'The Personal Social Services: Everyone's poor relation but nobody's baby,' in John Hills, ed., *The State of Welfare*, Clarendon Press, 1990, p. 233.

14 National Audit Office, October 1989, *op. cit,* p. 4.

Chapter 9: Conclusion

1 *A Child in Trust*, Brent, *op. cit.*

2 Linda Challis, University of Bath, personal communication, April 1992.

3 University of Bath, Centre for the Analysis of Social Policy, *Review of Consolidation in Brent Social Services, Summary of the Final Report*, July, 1987, p. 2.

Chapter 10: Recommendations

1 Rao, 1991, *op. cit.,* pp. 67-68.

2 Neill, 1991, *op. cit.*

3 BMA, 1992, *op. cit.,* pp. 41-44.

4 Colin Godber and Joan Higgins, 'Antithesis to the Past,' *The Health Services Journal*, 15 March, 1990, p. 399; BMA, 1992, *op. cit.,* para. 2.60.

5 Richard Berthoud, 'Meeting the Costs of Disability', in Gillian Dalley, ed., *Disability and Social Policy*, Policy Studies Institute, 1991.

6 Schorr, 1986, *op. cit.,* p.63.

7 But see Richard Berthoud, 'Using Benefits to Pay for Care at Home', in Baldwin, 1988, *op. cit.*; Berthoud, 1991, *op. cit.*; Christine Oldman, Presentation at STICERD seminar, London School of Economics, 18 February, 1992.

8 *Local Authority Expenditure, 1992/93, Personal Social Services, England*, Local Authority Associations, June, 1991.

9 Utting, 1991, *op. cit.*

10 Charles Carter with Peter John, *A New Accord*, Joseph Rowntree Foundation, 1992.

11 Packman, 1991, *op. cit.,* p. 324.